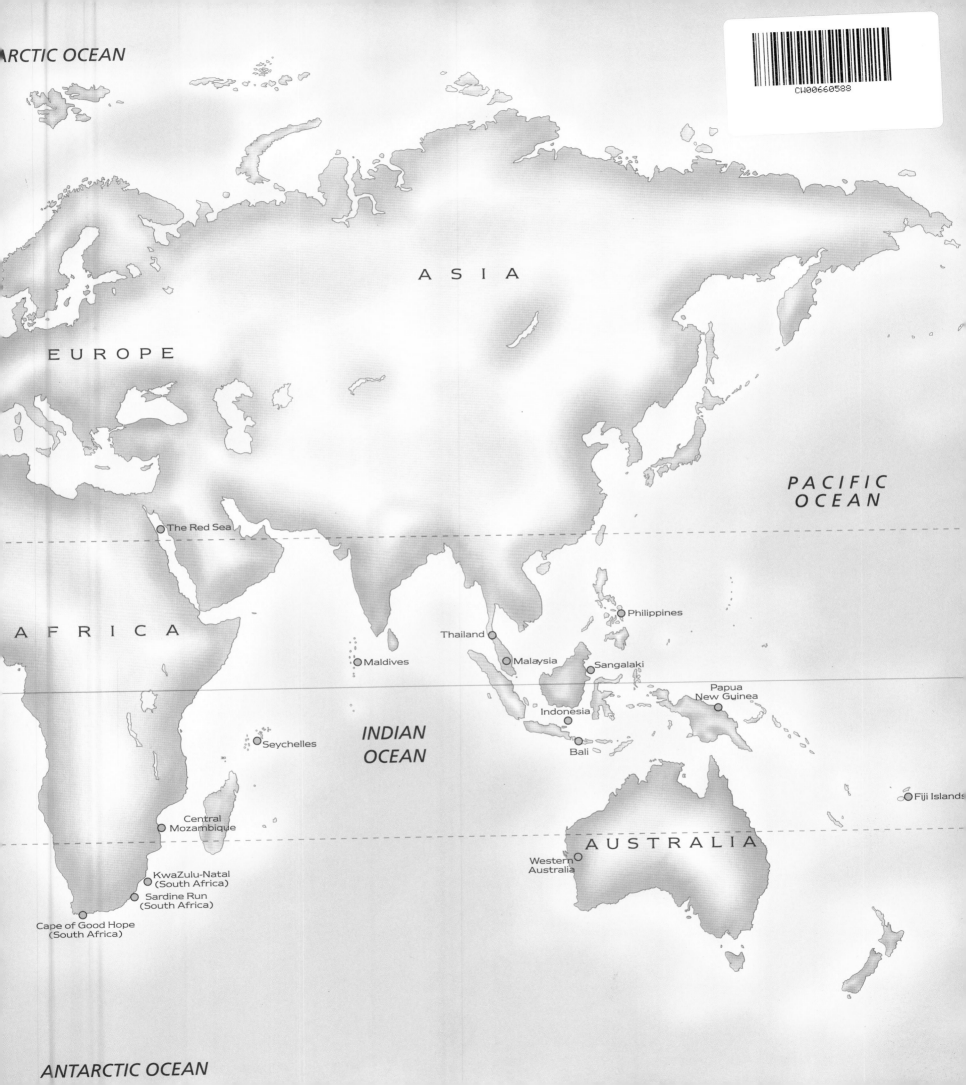

ARCTIC OCEAN

ASIA

EUROPE

PACIFIC
OCEAN

The Red Sea

AFRICA

Philippines

Thailand

Maldives

Malaysia

Sangalaki

Papua
New Guinea

Indonesia

INDIAN
OCEAN

Seychelles

Bali

Fiji Islands

Central
Mozambique

AUSTRALIA

Western
Australia

KwaZulu-Natal
(South Africa)

Sardine Run
(South Africa)

Cape of Good Hope
(South Africa)

ANTARCTIC OCEAN

DIVING WITH GIANTS

DIVING WITH GIANTS

CONSULTANT EDITOR Jack Jackson

NEW HOLLAND

First published in 2006 by New Holland Publishers
London • Cape Town • Sydney • Auckland
www.newhollandpublishers.com

86 Edgware Road
London
W2 2EA
United Kingdom

14 Aquatic Drive
Frenchs Forest
NSW 2086
Australia

80 McKenzie Street
Cape town
8001
South Africa

218 Lake Road
Northcote
Auckland
New Zealand

Disclaimer : The author and publishers have made every effort to
ensure that the information contained in this book was accurate at
the time of going to press, and accept no responsibility for any injury
or inconvenience sustained by any person using this book or following the advice provided herein.

Publishing Managers : Claudia Dos Santos, Simon Pooley
Commissioning Editor: Alfred LeMaitre
Editor: Rod Baker
Designer: Christelle Marais
Picture Research: Tamlyn Beaumont-Thomas
Cartography: Ryan Africa
Production: Myrna Collins
Consultant: Jack Jackson

ISBN 1 84537 180 1

Reproduction by Resolution Colour (Pty) Ltd, Cape Town
Printed and bound in Singapore by Tien Wah Press (Pte) Ltd

10 9 8 7 6 5 4 3 2 1

C O N T E N T S

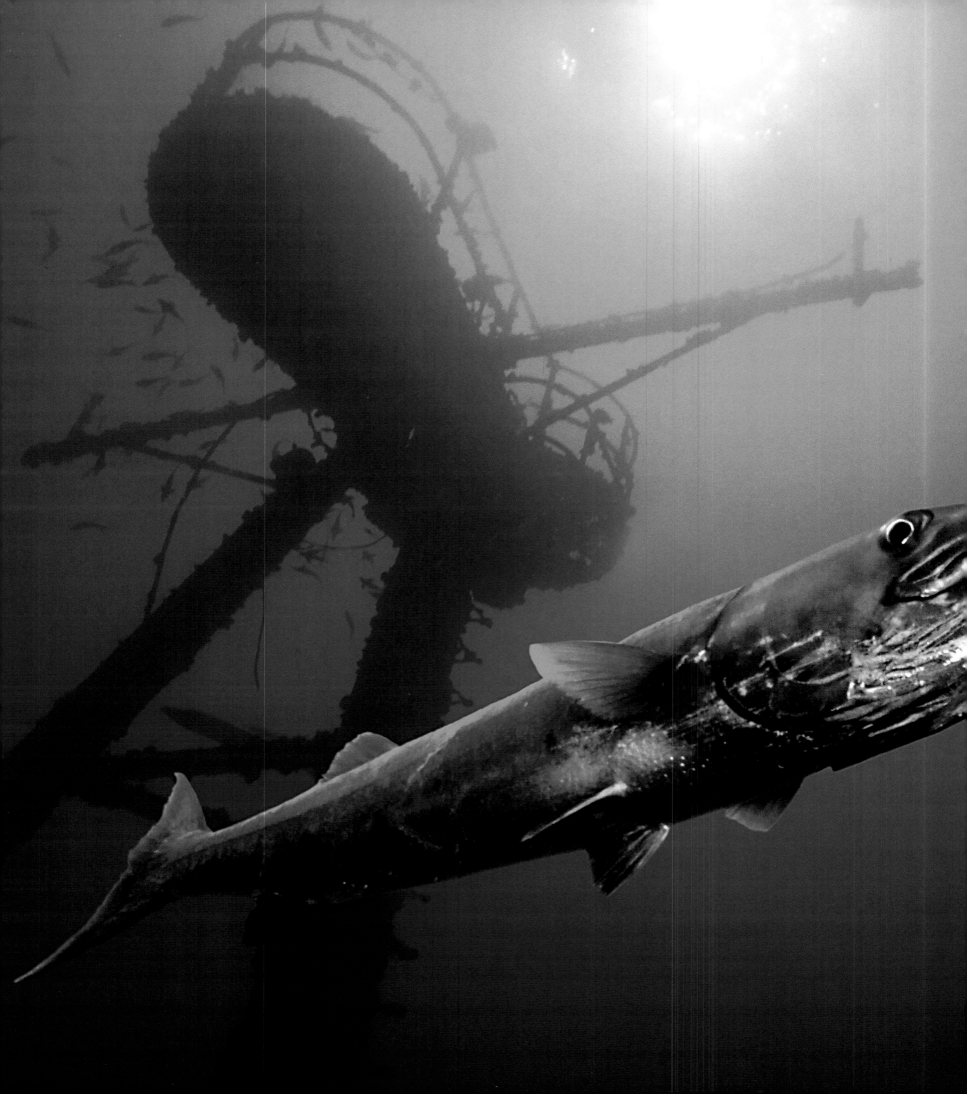

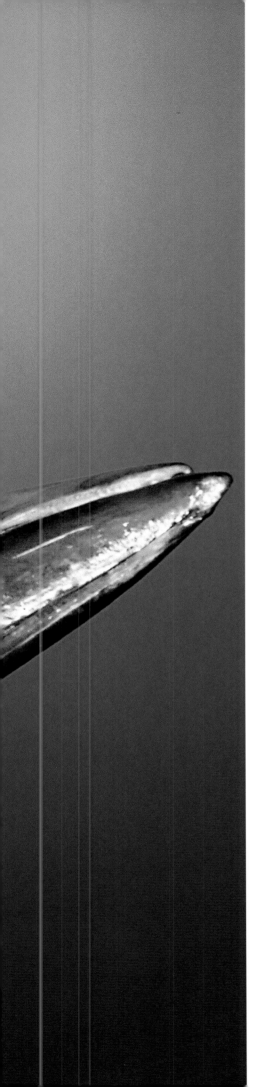

INTRODUCTION

Jack Jackson

Diving with large pelagic species is an experience that fills one with both awe and respect. Swimming with a Whale Shark as big as a bus gives one a feeling of amazement that this magnificent animal can reach such a size, but at the same time, it is hard to believe that it is completely non-threatening even though you know that it is a filter feeder, eating plankton and small fish. Similar filter feeders such as Basking Sharks are not much smaller and the larger Manta Rays 'flying' overhead are a similarly impressive but non-threatening sight. Most pelagic species are not large so divers tend to ignore them and consider pelagic animals to mainly be the larger species from large barracuda, through marlin, sharks, Manta Rays, Orcas, Basking and Whale Sharks to whales.

Left *Great Barracuda are the largest of the barracuda species; they are usually found alone or in small groups.*

Pollution and plundering

When it comes to conservation, pollution is generally not a major problem in the open sea except for plastic bags, which some turtles mistake for jellyfish. If a plastic bag is swallowed, the turtle's digestive system may be blocked and the animal will starve to death.

Most countries protect the fish stocks within their territorial limits but unless special treaties have been agreed, they cannot stop the plunder of fish stocks in international waters. For example, the temperate waters around the UK once used to teem with fish; cod and other fish were the cheap food for the masses. Now, however, cod stocks have collapsed through over-fishing, and meat can be cheaper than fish.

Practices such as pair trawling and long line fishing have terrible effects due to the by-catch of dolphins and birds, while bottom trawling destroys the seabed. This, together with oil and gas exploration and extraction, removes deep-water corals (also called cold-water corals) that are thousands of years old and have formed reefs or 'mounds' that are crucial habitats for commercially important fish and invertebrates.

In northwest Africa, local subsistence fishermen starve while large EU fishing fleets plunder their waters with licences bought from their governments.

Migration

In common with many land animals and birds, some pelagic fish make long migrations and this enables divers to predict where they might be found at particular times of year. Euryhaline fish – those that can tolerate both salt and fresh water – such as salmon, eels, and Bull (Zambezi) Sharks, make long journeys and spend some of their life in rivers. For instance, the European Eels found in the UK's Thames Estuary spawn in the Sargasso Sea in the heart of the Bermuda Triangle and then drift in the Gulf Stream

to Europe, where they reach adulthood in rivers such as the Thames.

Turtles also cover large areas. Some get caught up in the Gulf Stream and like some Ocean Sunfish, turn up off the west coast of the UK. In an ideal situation, any female turtle would return to its beach of birth to lay its eggs but many beaches get ruined naturally or we build on them. When this happens, some turtles have shown that they can adapt and use another beach.

Tuna tagged in American waters are caught off Japan, and a Tiger Shark tagged off Hawaii was caught in Mexico's Sea of Cortez.

Whale Sharks, which migrate to feed on plankton, somehow know when corals spawn at certain locations such as Ningaloo

Reef, Western Australia, and unusually, some feed on the spawn of Cubera Snappers off Gladden Spit, Belize.

Some whales make long migrations from temperate to warm water. Humpback Whales mate and calve in tropical waters during the winter and then travel to cold, polar waters during the summer to feed. While in warm waters the adults do not eat, but live off their layer of blubber. The young calves feed on rich mother's milk. Grey Whales make a very long migration; they feed in the cold waters of the Arctic Ocean northwest of Alaska and migrate along the coast to calve and mate in the warm, protected lagoons of the Pacific Ocean off Baja, Mexico.

Field studies on California's Farallon Islands and South Africa's Dyer Island show that

some Great White Sharks return annually. However, most tagged sharks are never seen again, a testimony to their nomadic lifestyle. Although primarily occupying and migrating within continental and insular shelf habitats, some larger Great White Sharks cross great ocean basins. Recently a female Great White of nearly 4m (13ft) was tagged off Gansbaai, southeast of Cape Town, South Africa, and the pop-off tag detached itself off Australia's Northwest Cape near Exmouth. Off

Australia a Great White Shark tagged in the Neptune Islands swam 7000km (4340 miles) to Rockhampton in Queensland and back to the Neptune Islands in less than a year.

Blue Sharks also traverse ocean basins, making long journeys in the Atlantic and Pacific and some cross the equator. Tagging indicates that they travel with the seasons as the water cools. Many fish have a preferred temperature range, and thus they change depths between night and day or area between summer and winter or if El Niño causes water temperatures to change. Some ocean animals make regular daily journeys between various feeding grounds and the depths and other parts of their realm. For instance, schools of Scalloped Hammerheads such as those at Cocos and Malpelo

make regular journeys along the same route during the day and night.

Scalloped Hammerheads at Sanganeb Reef in the Sudanese Red Sea will be in schools of over 100 at the North Point in the early morning. Then they break into groups of 10 or so and some travel along the East Face to arrive at the Southwest Point by 14:00 each afternoon. Plankton feeders, such as Basking Sharks and Manta Rays, follow the plankton as it rises to the surface in the afternoon.

Natural navigators

Some animals and birds apparently navigate using magnetic field lines. Pigeons, for example, possess a magnetic mineral called magnetite in their bodies but sharks do not, so it is possible that they employ the electroreceptors in their heads instead. In experiments using artificial magnetic fields, marine biologists have confirmed that some sharks can detect changes in the fields. Moreover, Tiger, Blue and Scalloped Hammerhead Sharks are all known to swim in straight lines across great expanses of open ocean, and then orient themselves to seamounts where geomagnetic anomalies exist.

The earth's magnetic field changes slowly over time and in billions of years of geological time it has reversed occasionally. However, earthquakes can cause slight but sudden modifications to magnetic field lines and fool animals. At least one scientist theorizes that this could be the cause of some whale and dolphin strandings.

Up close

It is actually quite rare for those that are not accredited researchers to dive or snorkel in fully open water but there are a few operators who specialize in this, including those who use cages to keep the divers safe from dangerous sharks. With Whale Sharks, some whales and Basking Sharks, it is normal to drop snorkellers ahead of the animal in the direction that it is travelling. Spotter planes are often used to find Whale Sharks and tell the operator by radio where to drop the snorkellers.

Environmentalists soon realized, however, that in popular areas such as Ningaloo Reef, some divers were harassing the animals, so now no-one is allowed to dive with, touch or otherwise interfere with the animals. Snorkelling may

be allowed but flash photography is prohibited. Similar rules exist for diving or snorkelling with whales and dolphins, but there are a few countries where there are still no restrictions.

Many animals are attracted to floating objects so scuba diving for pelagics is often carried out around buoys anchored in deep water. Another system that works well in deep water is dropping the anchor line or other weighted-line from the boat and dive around

Opposite *The speed and power of a Great White Shark when it attacks from below often takes it well out of the water.*

Below *Even from the deck of a boat, the massive size of a Great White Shark will impress people.*

fish such as marlin or sailfish is a challenge; I have seen a sluggish sailfish in the poor visibility of a lagoon but this fish was probably ill. They normally move very quickly in open water. Fish like this are 'fought' on a sport-angler's line until brought to the boat exhausted, then they can be released and filmed or photographed before they recover enough to swim away.

Most sharks are not dangerous to man and some can be sent into a torpid state. Silvertip Sharks, for example, will go into a torpid state if turned upside down. Similarly, when caught or placed under stress, captured Tiger Sharks will struggle at first but then go into a torpid state and it takes some time for them to recover. This technique has been used in the making of some feature films: the shark is released to swim lethargically along a set course for the shot and recaptured before it can recover. This is why these sharks look clumsy in such films. Off South Africa, there is at least one operator who cups his hand around a Great White Shark's nose when it raises its head above the surface beside the boat. The animal pauses, seemingly transfixed for a few seconds, before submerging again.

it to a safe depth while the boat drifts. With both of these types of diving it is necessary to have a point of reference and the easiest way to achieve this is for the divers to attach themselves to the anchor line, shotline or line to the buoy with a Jon line (see p17).

Diving off coral reefs, rocks or seamounts that are surrounded by large expanses of deep water is more common. In these places, when the currents hit the reef, rock or seamount, any upwellings that they cause bring up a good supply of nutrients from the depths. Similar situations are found at the exits of channels that discharge nutrients from lagoons with the ebbing tide. These nutrients feed smaller creatures, which in turn attract larger pelagic species.

To bait, or not to bait

With very few lucky exceptions, all predatory shark photographs are taken with the help of baiting, chumming or feeding – whatever you wish to call it. The scent of the bait is carried downstream on the current and the stronger the current, the farther the scent is carried. At first those reef sharks that are closest will come to the bait, but if you wait a while pelagic sharks from greater distances will arrive to investigate. Where cages are used, some of the bait is pulled to the cage to help the photographers get their pictures.

In some research or filming situations, small boats can approach a natural kill and the scene is photographed, videoed or filmed using a remotely controlled unit with a camera or a Polecam (a camera attached to a pole) lowered into the water from the boat. No divers or snorkellers are in the water so there is no danger and any animal behaviour is natural. In addition, video cameras are now becoming so small that they can be tagged to the dorsal fins of living sharks. They operate as the shark swims along and then detach and float to the surface for retrieval after a certain period.

Researchers have filmed breaching Great White Sharks in South Africa by towing a model of a seal pup along the surface. Photographing naturally swimming game

Diving safety

Always dive conservatively, especially where it is not possible to reach a recompression (hyperbaric) chamber. Where one exists, ensure beforehand that you know how to contact it or the relevant authorities that control either its use or the evacuation procedures to reach it. Do not assume that the nearest recompression (hyperbaric) chamber is the most appropriate one for treatment. Check first.

Using electrical discharges to repel sharks

Sharks have a sensory system called the Ampullae de Lorenzini – gel-filled canals connecting the surface of the snout to the nervous system – that are sensitive to the tiny electrical impulses generated by muscle movement in all animals. Predatory sharks home in on their prey by sight, smell and pressure waves but when they get close some protect their eyes with a nictitating membrane or, in the case of Great Whites, roll their eyes backwards, and use their Ampullae de Lorenzini in the final stage of the attack. This system is particularly useful when prey is buried in the sand.

However, other objects that produce electricity or affect the electrical field can fool the system – which is why Great Whites sometimes mouth metal boats and propellers.

The Natal Sharks Board, a South African government agency created to protect divers, surfers and swimmers while preserving the shark population, researched electronic devices to reduce shark attacks. Experimenting with a device patented in America in 1962 they worked out the characteristics of the pulsing electric field most disliked by the more dangerous sharks, the Great White, Tiger, Bull and Oceanic Whitetip. They then incorporated it into a battery-powered unit marketed in 1995 as the 'Shark POD' (Protective Oceanic Device).

The battery pack and one electrode are strapped to the diver's scuba cylinder and another electrode is attached to one of the diver's fins. The cable with the on/off switch is brought over the shoulder for accessibility. The elliptical electrical field created repels sharks at between one and seven metres without affecting other creatures, though divers have felt shocks in metal fillings. The unit is not effective in fresh water because fresh water will not conduct the electrical current. Similarly, both electrodes must be in the water to complete the circuit for the system to work.

In January 2002, an Australian company, SeaChange Technology, acquired an exclusive licence to produce smaller, cheaper and more energy-efficient versions, which they marketed under the name 'Shark Shield'.

There are different models designed for divers, snorkellers, swimmers, surfers, windsurfers, kayakers and so on. The Australian military and police forces use them.

Dangerous changes

However, changes to a local environment can cause more dangerous behaviour: fishermen cleaning their catch and throwing the unwanted fish-parts into the water will attract sharks, as will abattoirs that discharge waste into the sea. Schools of fish may be driven inshore by currents or changes in water temperatures and sharks that feed on them may bite swimmers or surfers. In some Third World countries people use harbours or beaches as bathrooms and children splashing about in the shallows can attract small sharks. In poor visibility a wrist, leg or ankle may look very much like their normal prey. There has been a spate of shark attacks along a 20km (12.4 mile) stretch of the Brazilian coast since a new port blocked two fresh-water estuaries where female Bull Sharks used to give birth. It is believed that many of these females then moved to the next estuary, which discharges onto the stretch of beach where the attacks are occurring.

There are many places where larger animals can be observed without observers entering the water at all. Whales and Basking Sharks are watched from high cliffs when close to shore and whales and Great White Sharks can be observed from high points on the Farallon Islands.

Ecological and ethical diving

The growing awareness of environmental issues has given rise to 'ecotourism' – managing tourism and tourists in an ecologically sustainable way. The capital investment necessary to develop ecotourism is minimal, much-needed employment is created for the local population and in the long term the profits exceed those of logging or overfishing.

Although many divers, dive operators and diving resorts lead the field in protecting marine ecosystems, we all need somewhere to eat and sleep. If a small resort is built without a waste-treatment system, the nearby reefs may still not be seriously damaged. However, if those same reefs attract increasing numbers of tourists and further resorts, then controls become necessary. Environmentalists can go too far, however.

If the rules in one area are too strict, operators may be forced to give up as divers and snorkellers go elsewhere. Without divers and snorkellers around to keep an eye on the animals and if local people do not gain employment from tourism, there is more chance of fishermen using destructive fishing methods or fishing out the animals concerned.

Damage done unwittingly by divers also concerns many people. Hence, keeping the popular areas of the marine environment ecologically sustainable depends as much on divers as it does on the operators and resorts.

Ethical diving practices

- Be properly weighted and master good buoyancy control; you can kill coral simply by touching it while trying to maintain your position. Also important is the amount of physical energy you save by having the correct buoyancy.

- Tuck in all equipment to stop it touching any marine animals.

- If you are about to collide with the reef, steady yourself with your fingertips on a part of the reef that is already dead.

- Do not use deep fin-strokes next to the reef, the surge of water stresses delicate organisms and disturbed sand smothers corals by settling on them.

- Except on wrecks, do not wear gloves in warm waters. This will help you avoid holding onto live corals or touching the animals.

- Do not hitch rides on any sea animal.

- Do not collect or purchase marine souvenirs.

- Before booking a dive trip on a boat, ask about the operator's environmental policy and avoid boats that are known to cause unnecessary anchor damage, have bad oil leaks, or discharge untreated sewage near reefs.

- On any excursion, whether with an operator or privately organized, make sure you take your garbage back for proper disposal on land.

- Do not spear-fish for sport. Selective killing of the larger fish upsets the reproductive chain and the natural balance. If you are living on a boat and relying on spear-fishing for food, make sure you are familiar with all local fish and game regulations and obtain the necessary licences.

- Night diving requires extra care; strong lights dazzle and confuse animals so avoid pointing bright lights directly at them.

The ethics of feeding

Conservationists argue that feeding fish alters their natural feeding behaviour, affects their health, makes them dependent on divers and could attract more dangerous predators. They have a point with regard to feeding Humphead (Napoleon) Wrasse with eggs, or any fish with food that is not part of its natural diet. But others argue that feeding does not alter long-term behaviour.

Most animals are opportunistic feeders, not averse to carrion, and the amount of food that divers introduce is minimal so the fish do not become reliant on it. At the Cayman Island's Stingray City, the rays are fed many times each day, yet are still observed feeding naturally. At

shark-feeds elsewhere a few dominant animals monopolize the food while most of the others go without. More importantly, the number of divers that these themed events attract has led governments to realize that the animals are worth more when kept alive for tourism than wiped out by fishermen. It is estimated that half of the diving/snorkelling dollars spent in Grand Cayman are on the Southern Stingray feeds and that in the Bahamas, shark feeds bring in over US$60m a year.

However, things must be kept in perspective. Shark attacks have occurred in areas where no feeding occurs and there has not been any obvious reason for these attacks. When wearing light-coloured fins, I have had them bitten by both large groupers and sharks, although no feeding had previously occurred at the dive sites concerned. The most likely inference is that the larger fish mistook the fins to be smaller, prey-sized fish. A large barracuda once attacked me in water with very poor visibility; I was using a camera at the time so it is likely that a glint of sun on the lens looked like the flash of a small silver fish – the barracuda's normal prey.

I personally know three divers who have been bitten by sharks while they were too close to bait balls on which the predators were feeding. There are several well-known operators who have been bitten by groupers or moray eels that they fed regularly, but at the time of the incidents they were feeding other fish. In addition, several people have suffered small grazes at organized shark-feeds in the Bahamas.

However, even where hundreds of non-cage shark-feeds are performed yearly with hand-feeding and/or large amounts of bait, there have been very few injuries, and those that did occur were mostly to those actually performing the hand-feeding. When shark attacks do occur on spear-fishermen, they are usually still carrying dead or – worse still – fish thrashing about in their death throes.

So eventually, by the law of averages a tourist will suffer a serious injury or die during a feeding operation. However, the incident-rate is well within the range of adventure sports in general and considerably safer than mountaineering, skiing or snowboarding – and way below the number of people killed by bee stings or lightning.

Be responsible

With reference to feeding sharks, some species are more belligerent than others, and Grey Reef Sharks are known to be more belligerent in some areas than they are in others. Having regularly organized shark-feeds in the Red Sea since the early 1980s, my own feeling is that many operators use too much bait. A couple of 25cm (10in) fish hidden in the coral are enough to keep the sharks interested for 20 minutes. I also think that it is better not to hand-feed, even with chain-mail gloves, as this gives the sharks the impression that man supplies the food, and this could possibly lead to a situation where sharks harass divers who are not involved in feeding.

If carried out in a responsible manner, shark-feeding dives are reasonably safe. As divers we are privileged to have remarkably close encounters with wildlife underwater, often within arm's length, though not everyone wants to get this close to a shark. However, there have been many instances where, without any connection to feeding, other animals such as large barracuda, large groupers, moray eels and even Titan or Yellowmargin Triggerfish have either bitten or butted divers and caused injuries. Feeding fish is an emotive issue – you must make up your own mind.

Jon line (general utility and buddy-line)

A Jon line is a 2 or 4m (6 or 13ft) length of strong line, 25mm (1in) tape or bungee cord with any number of uses including that of a buddy-line. It is connected to the diver with a karabiner (snaplink) and the other end has a special spring clip that will securely lock round a rope, anchor chain or shotline with one-hand operation.

If the current is strong while the divers are descending, they can loosely wrap their Jon line around the anchor line or shotline so that they do not get swept away. When ascending, a Jon line is ideal for safety stops or decompression stops as it enables divers to hang on to an anchor line or shotline with hands-free attachment and is particularly useful where several divers are holding the same depth at the same time.

Some divers prefer a Jon line made from bungee cord because it takes up the shock and much of the movement while attached to an anchor line or shotline of a boat or buoy that is bouncing around in a swell. Instead of using a clip on the anchor line you can use a short loop of line to form a mountaineer's prusik knot and clip to that. You can easily move this along the anchor line by hand to change your depth.

You can also imitate a prusik knot with the end of the line: wrap the end several times around the anchor line, pull it tight and knot it, then use a karabiner to clip the line to itself. Jon lines were named after the originator, Jon Hulbert.

Above *A Great White Shark is lured to the boat by bait on a line.*

Technical and safety issues

Where divers or snorkellers are to be in open water from a boat it is particularly important that they are very fit, not overweight, and have a foolproof check-out and check-back-in procedure so that the boat crew always knows if somebody is still in the water. Divers should also have orange or yellow surface marker buoys, rescue sausages or flags and other signalling devices so that the boat can find them easily when they are spread out.

As an ex-boat skipper, I advise divers/snorkellers not to wear black or dark blue exposure suits or buoyancy control devices (BCDs) as these are difficult for the main or chase boat crew to see.

With larger animals that swim near to the surface there are definite advantages with snorkelling rather than using scuba equipment. When the animals are located, the boat may have to travel some distance to get into position and once it is in position, it is important to enter the water quickly but quietly. The animals are not spooked by the sound of scuba exhaust bubbles and without the drag of scuba equipment you can swim much faster. Moreover, Manta Rays are often curious of snorkellers and keep returning to them.

People snorkelling in a sunny climate should wear an exposure suit or old jeans and T-shirt for protection against sunburn as the back, neck and back of the knees can be particularly painful if sunburnt. Whale and Orca encounters can be in water that is cold enough for 7mm (9/32in) wet or semi-dry suits or dry suits.

Snorkelling sounds ideal for beginners but this is not so in open water, where it is easy to

Dive flags

The official flag that covers both professional and sport diving is the maritime International Code of Signals 'A' Flag.

When flown on its own, the 'A' Flag signifies that a vessel has divers in the water so other craft should keep clear and reduce speed. It is illegal to fly this flag if the vessel concerned does not actually have divers in the water at the time the flag is displayed.

American recreational divers have produced their own diving flag; this one does not have any legal international meaning and will often be flown outside diving establishments and on vessels that do not have divers in the water. Some diving operators or shops add their own logo to this flag.

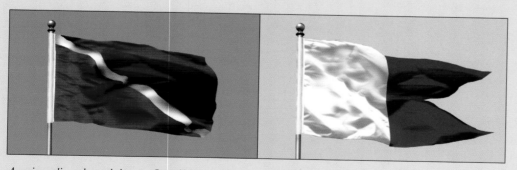

American divers have their own flag. Although it has no legal status, it is widely used by diving operators.

The internationally recognized 'A' flag signifies that a boat has divers in the water.

BCD colour

There is a tendency for the modern buoyancy control device (BCD) to be black. As a boat captain who is definitely not colour blind, I had difficulty picking out divers in black or blue BCDs at a distance on drift dives. In fact, if the divers were not using a surface marker buoy the glint of the sun on a mask or a sunburned face was often more obvious. So, be aware that divers are more easily spotted if they wear an orange or yellow coloured BCD.

Although research has shown that bright yellow is the colour spotted most easily, fishermen find that bright orange is the best colour for buoys etc. floating on the water surface.

become disorientated. Only very experienced snorkellers or divers who have passed a PADI Advanced Open Water Diver, BS-AC Club Diver/Ocean Diver or equivalent course should engage in this. The same level of diving training is recommended for those shark-feeds where the divers are not in a protective cage.

Some non-cage shark-feed operators insist that divers wear dark-coloured gloves and keep their hands still and close to the body because their hands may look like edible-sized fish to the sharks. It is also advisable to avoid light-coloured fins as they too may be mistaken for prey.

Cage-diving

In cages at the surface some people just use a mask and snorkel so they do not need to be a scuba diver or have any scuba qualification, but if using scuba equipment, it is an advantage to have a basic open water certification. Divers in a cage may be supplied with air from an air compressor on the boat instead of wearing a BCD and cylinder. This is known as surface-supply or the 'hookah system', with the air being supplied through an extended hose.

If the cage is floating on the surface, it will tend to bounce around in any swell, so seasickness is possible.

In the majority of instances where cages are used, divers will require 7mm (9/32in) wet or semi-dry suits or dry suits, should carry more lead weights than they actually need to keep them steady on the cage floor, and should not wear fins. With most

Above *Although the situation is exaggerated by bait being drawn along the surface, few sensible people would want to be here without the protection of a cage.*

operators, when the sharks appear the clients spend time in the cages in strict rotation. This, combined with the temperature of the water, limits how long they spend in the cage at any one time. There can also be long periods of waiting in the boat and the weather may not always be good. So, be prepared with warm, windproof and water-proof clothing, a hat, high-SPF (sun protection factor) anti-sunburn lotion, motion sickness tablets, camera, and a towel.

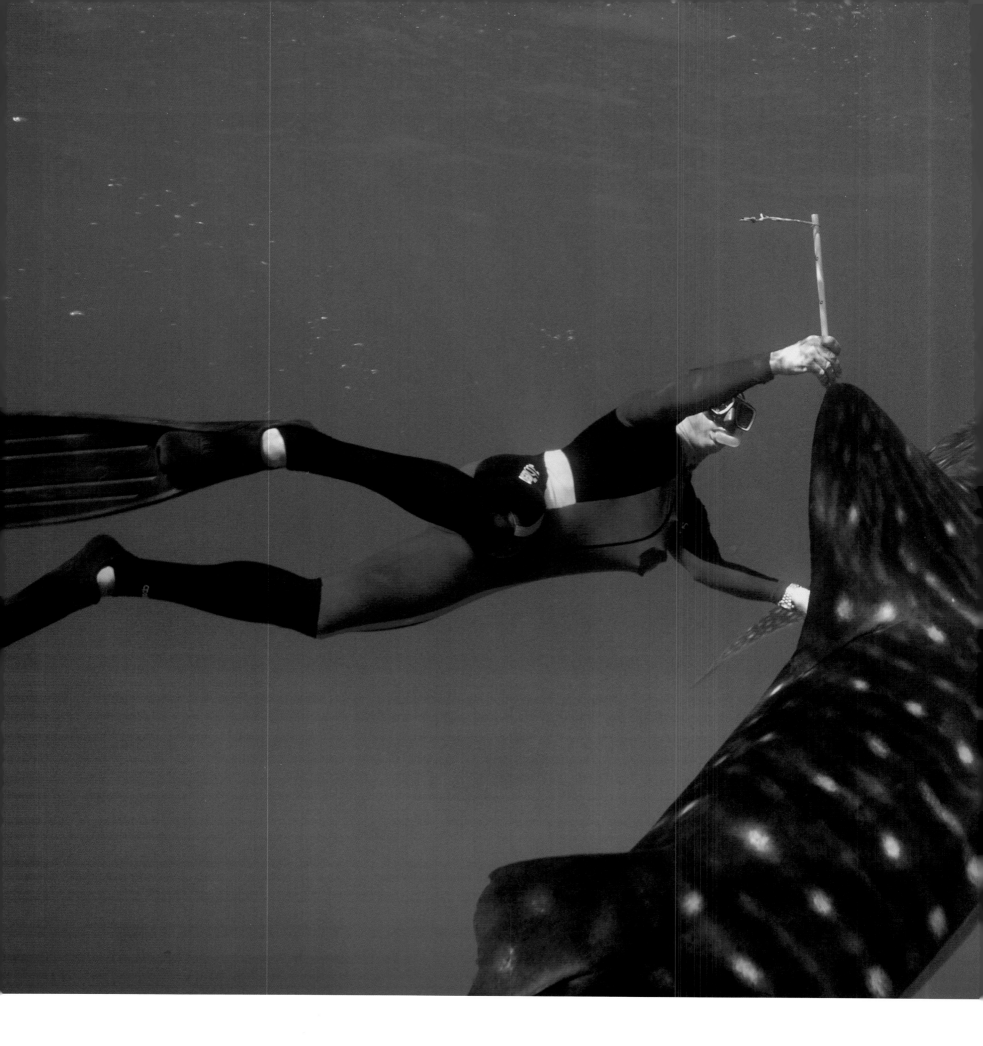

Tagged Whale Sharks 'surprise' scientists

When researchers from the Australian Institute of Marine Science (AIMS) tagged Whale Sharks off Western Australia's Ningaloo Reef recently, they found that although they were prolific swimmers and dove over a kilometre down, there was no set pattern to their travels.

Two sharks stayed around Ningaloo for two months before leaving, one stayed around Indonesian Java for two weeks and two others swam up towards Christmas Island and then out into the open Indian Ocean.

Left *The tags attached to Whale Sharks provide a wealth of information, such as the depths to which the creatures dive – though scientists still do not know why they dive so deep.*

Tagging and tracking Great Whites

CSIRO Marine Research (CMR), part of the largest marine research organization in Australia, the Commonwealth Scientific and Industrial Research Organisation (CSIRO), has been tagging Great White Sharks with electronic tags that can transmit their position and other parameters to the ARGOS satellite system.

To conserve the battery, each tag – which is attached to the shark's dorsal fin – is fitted with a saltwater switch. While the animal is submerged the device is off, but as soon as the shark surfaces and the switch is clear of the water, it activates the tag, which transmits a signal to satellites. These in turn relay the position to a ground station in France and CSIRO scientists then use this data to plot the shark's movements, accurate to 120m (394ft).

A male shark nicknamed 'Bruce' made one of the longest journeys tracked to date – more than 6000km (3728 miles). Originally tagged off the Neptune Islands, 50km (31 miles) south of Port Lincoln in March 2004, Bruce remained around the Neptune Islands for several days before travelling south and then east through the Bass Strait, then north along the coast of Victoria during April and May. He then continued north along the New South Wales coast, entering the waters of southern Queensland in June.

He then moved up to Rockhampton, and spent September and October both off the continental shelf east of Rockhampton and in inshore waters before starting south again. He was last pinpointed near the northern Victorian coastline in November, just before the battery of his satellite tag ran out.

However, he later returned to the Neptune Islands, where charter boat skipper Rolf Czabayski, one of those involved in his tagging with the CSIRO, instantly recognized this ocean traveller.

Pelagic Species Guide

Listing the larger species that are dived or snorkelled with would fill this book so here is just a selection of the more interesting ones:

Baleen whales

Blue Whales are the largest and loudest animals that have ever lived. Reaching a length of 30m (98ft), and with a call level of up to 188 decibels, they feed on plankton, krill (shrimp-like animals, which form enormous schools), and small fish.

Grey Whales are benthic (bottom) feeders, and have a sharp beak, large, muscular tongue and short, stiff baleen plates. They stir up the bottom sediment and sieve mouthfuls of mud for crustaceans and molluscs. They reach a length of 15m (49ft).

Humpback Whales produce the longest and most varied 'songs' in the animal world, and employ complex, co-operative 'bubble-net' feeding techniques. Reaching 17.5m (57ft) they eat plankton, krill and small fish. They breach and slap their fins and flukes on the water, are not afraid of boats and often allow snorkellers to get close.

Dwarf Minke Whales are among the smallest baleen whales. On the northern Great Barrier Reef drifting or anchored boats often intrigue them, and they may stay around for several hours in groups of up to 20. While many countries have now banned programmes where people can swim with whales, here an industry has developed based on voluntary approaches by these whales.

Above A Killer Whale or Orca breaching off Peninsula Valdez where they are present all year around.
Above left Loggerhead Turtles feed mostly on bottom-dwelling invertebrates.
Top right A juvenile Sperm Whale at the surface off the Azores.

Only known in the Southern Hemisphere, the largest Minke Whale that was accurately measured had a length of 7.8m (26ft). They feed on fish and krill.

Toothed whales

Orcas are powerful carnivores that eat fish both large and small, squid, and marine mammals. The largest dolphin, they live in small, life-long pods and are sometimes called

'wolves of the sea' because they hunt in packs. Reaching a length of 8m (26ft), Orcas are of two main types:

The transient Orca tends to wander about the ocean and preys on almost every animal in the sea including other whales, large baleen whales (for their tongues), plus hammerhead sharks and Basking Sharks.

The transient Orca is the one that intentionally beaches itself on the shores of Argentina to catch seal and sea lion pups.

Other Orcas remain local, preying on schooling fish such as salmon off British Columbia, and mackerel and herring off Norway, so these are safer to dive or snorkel with.

Pilot Whales are also dolphins and are second only to Orcas in size. There are two species, Longfin and Shortfin, and both have a distinct rounded head. Reaching 6m (20ft), they primarily eat squid but also take octopuses, cuttlefish, and small fish. They only have 40–48 teeth, compared with 120 or so of many other dolphin species.

Many of the larger species of dolphins readily approach divers; lone males can be too curious, even becoming sexually aroused.

Sharks and rays

The sharks that most interest divers fall into two main categories, the large Whale and Basking Sharks that eat plankton, and the larger of the predatory species including Blue, Bull, Great White, several species of hammerheads, mako, Oceanic Whitetip, Raggedtooth, Silky, Silvertip, and Tiger Sharks. Whale Sharks, the ocean's

Above When watching Great White Sharks from a cage you can get really close encounters.
Top left Blacktip Reef Sharks off French Polynesia.
Above left Often the first indication of a Manta Ray's presence is that the sun goes out.

largest fish, usually reach a length of 12m (39ft) and Basking Sharks can achieve 9m (30ft). Despite their reputation, Great White Sharks are rarely a length of over 5m (16ft), however. The largest ever documented was caught off Cuba and measured 6.4m (21 ft).

Rays are related to sharks and the largest, the graceful Manta Ray, can have a wingspan of 9m (30ft), which is more than twice its length. It feeds on microscopic plankton, small fish, and tiny crustaceans.

Best Dive Sites

Pelagic encounters where divers or snorkellers are actually in the water with the animal/s are mostly down to luck but they are most likely to see them in the following places where trips to see the animals are often organized.

Whale Sharks

Ningaloo Reef, Western Australia
Donsol, Philippines
Seychelles
Belize
Maldives
Thailand

Humpback Whales

French Polynesia

Basking Sharks

United Kingdom

Manta Rays

Maldives
Mozambique
Papua New Guinea
Tobago
Ningaloo Reef, Western Australia
Sangalaki
Hawaii
Thailand
Sudan
Cuba
Philippines

Dolphins

Egypt
Sudan

Ocean Sunfish

Bali, Indonesia
Azores
United Kingdom

Turtles

Pulau, Sangalaki
Kalimantan, Indonesia
Pulau Sipadan, Borneo, Malaysia
Turtle Islands Park, Sabah, Borneo
The Philippines
Bonaire
Grand Cayman Island

Great White Sharks

Guadalupe Island, Mexico
South Africa
South Australia

Mako Sharks

South Africa

Hammerhead sharks

Sudan
Bahamas
Sea of Cortez

Tiger Sharks

South Africa
Fiji

Raggedtooth Sharks

South Africa

Silvertip Sharks

Sudan
Papua New Guinea
French Polynesia
Naval buoy, Bahamas

Blue Sharks

South Africa

Right *Humpback Whales breaching while on their regular migration route.*

Above *Thanks to conservation and breeding programmes turtle species such as the Hawksbill, Green, Olive Ridley and Leatherback are far more common nowadays off islands such as the Caymans and Aruba, Bonaire and Curaçao.*

Caribbean & Atlantic

CUBA

One of diving's crown jewels

Jack Jackson

Shaped like a sleeping crocodile, Cuba straddles the confluence of the western tropical Atlantic and the Caribbean. It lies 145km (90 miles) south of Florida between Jamaica and the Bahamas, and has the Atlantic Ocean to the north and east, the Caribbean to the south and the Gulf of Mexico to the west. Cuba's 5746km (3563 mile) coast teems with marine life, making it perhaps the most prolific diving destination in the Caribbean – a biological crown jewel for fish, invertebrates and pelagics.

Cuba's Atlantic coast has a greater concentration of the colder water creatures but it also has Manta Rays. The areas at each end of Cuba have good mixtures of species, while the Caribbean coast has greater numbers of species.

South of Ciego de Avila, Los Jardines de la Reina (The Queen's Gardens), known to Americans as the Last Paradise Keys, is a chain of 250 uninhabited coral reefs stretching for over 160km (100 miles). Some 80km (50 miles) offshore, they are protected by the third-longest barrier reef in the world. As it's a marine park, access is restricted and commercial fishing is banned from all but the outermost extremes of the Park.

This area is known for its big fish including massive Goliath Groupers, Lemon, Silky and Bull Sharks.

Whale Sharks pass by in November and December. Most of the dive sites are protected from winds and currents, and visitors have the choice of a houseboat or live-aboard boats for their accommodation.

Whales and dolphins

There are at least 28 cetacean species in the area around Cuba:

Baleen whales, which filter their food such as krill and small shoaling fish through baleen-plates include Blue, Bryde's, Fin, Humpback, Minke, Northern Right and Sei.

The toothed whales found here include the following dolphins – Atlantic Bottlenose, Atlantic Spotted, Fraser's, Pan-tropical Spotted, Clymene, Risso's, Rough-toothed, Spinner and Striped – and the whales: Blainville's Beaked, Cuvier's Beaked, Gervais' Beaked, False Killer, Killer, Pygmy Killer, Shortfin Pilot, Melon-headed, Sowerby's Beaked, Pygmy Sperm, Dwarf Sperm and Sperm.

Humpback Whales, which breed in the region, are found migrating off northern Cuba and in the Gulf of Mexico.

The sharks

Whale Sharks are to be seen up and down the southern coast from August onwards, from September to November off María la Gorda and at Los Jardines de la Reina in November and December.

Right Loggerhead Turtles are among those that are less common in Cuban waters.

Opposite A dream for most divers and snorkellers is to get this close to a juvenile Great Sperm Whale.

Predatory pelagic sharks may be seen everywhere in Cuba, even large Great Whites were caught here in the late 1940s. Hammerhead, Blacktip, Bluntnose Six-gill, and Lemon Sharks are quite common everywhere but the best place to see pelagic sharks nowadays is at Los Jardines de la Reina. Here you will also find Silky and Bull Sharks, which are hand-fed. Occasionally a Great White passes through as well.

Mantas and turtles

Manta Rays are found all around Cuba, and several diving sites where they are often seen are named after them.

The waters around the island are also well known for their turtles.

The most common species in Cuba are Green and Hawksbill Turtles. Loggerheads are less common and Leatherbacks least of all.

All four of these species nest here, however. The Loggerhead Turtles usually inhabit river estuaries and lagoons in warm and temperate seas and oceans worldwide.

Ocean Sunfish

There are three species of Ocean Sunfish – the world's largest bony fish, but not its longest – and two are common in Cuban waters.

The most prevalent is the Roundtailed or Common Sunfish, which has a round tail and gritty, sandpapery skin covered in mucus. The other is the Sharptailed Sunfish, which has a more pronounced tail and a much smoother skin that produces less mucus. The latter grow as large as the former but 'sunbathe' less on the surface and carry fewer parasites.

Apart from its justified fame as a prime dive location in its own right, Cuba is also renowned for its role in the sport of game-fishing. The pastime is well organized in Cuba, and the usual Wahoo, Mahi Mahi, Bonito, tuna, marlin and sailfish can be found in offshore waters.

TOBAGO AND LITTLE CAYMAN

Meeting Manta Rays, the gentle giants

Lawson Wood

Manta Rays are actually more common in a number of Caribbean locations than we previously thought. The scuba-diving community nowadays is much more in touch with each other, so more people now know where to dive with these amazing creatures. At a dive site known as the Kelleston Drain, at Speyside, Tobago, rays are seen in about 75 per cent of all dives. These massive delta-winged fish are quite graceful, but very fast, so keeping up with them can be a challenge. Fortunately, however, the strong currents of this particular dive off Tobago are such that you are able to keep up with the mantas for a thrilling experience.

Over a decade ago, for a period of over 18 months, Little Cayman Island was very special. It was the only location known in the Caribbean where you could sit on the seabed each night in 10m (33ft) of water, switch on your dive lights and sit in stunned awe as a particular female Manta Ray swooped in and performed barrel-rolls in front of you.

This female was, of course, scooping up krill and other plankton attracted by the dive lights, but her regular appearances meant she soon became well known and a 'must see' attraction.

During the dive briefing before entering the water that first night, we were a little sceptical of what we had been told. The intention was to dive down to an area known as Eagle Ray Round Up, where there was a heavy enough mooring buoy to secure our diving vessel. All of the divers had to form a semicircle and point their dive lights into its centre. We were told that we would perhaps have to wait up to 15 minutes before the Manta Ray showed up.

We descended but no sooner had we landed on the sand than the ray swooped in, surprising us. There was a flurry of flashes as everyone vied for the best position and it soon became clear that the manta, known locally as 'Molly', had trained *us*. Her wingspan of over 3m (10ft) made an impressive sight as she performed in front of each diver. The stronger the lights, the more plankton and krill was attracted and subsequently the more Molly would feed in front of you. Sadly, she is no longer around, but perhaps one of her descendants, or another ray, will take her place one day.

Mantas feed by extending the fleshy lobes on each side of their mouth, channelling the flow of plankton towards the cavernous mouth. The lobes are retracted when the ray is not feeding.

Looking very closely at this amazingly graceful creature, you can see every gill opening, and every detail of the inside of the mouth.

I have also personally encountered Manta Rays off Honduras and the Bahamas, but they are known from the Netherlands Antilles, the Grenadines and Cuba.

Right *While feeding a manta will extend its cephalic lobes, which direct food into its mouth.*

Opposite *To have a Manta Ray soaring overhead, blotting out the sun's rays is genuinely awesome.*

Top right *One of the most graceful oceanic wanderers, Manta Rays are often found at the edge of coral reefs where they await their turn at 'cleaning stations'.*

ARUBA, BONAIRE & CURAÇAO
Where the turtles rule

Jack Jackson

The islands of Aruba, Bonaire and Curaçao are outside the hurricane belt so they are all-year-round destinations. Operators combine day-boat dives with unlimited shore dives but you should note that none of the diving operators on Aruba allow solo diving, though the Habitat Resorts on both Bonaire and Curaçao do. In the autumn, coral spawning around September and October is a big event on all three islands.

Because the constant Trade Winds cause rough seas, most of the diving on all three islands is on leeward sites and as a result, although Scalloped Hammerhead, Lemon and nurse sharks are seen, divers tend to think that the large pelagics are not found here. However, coral spawning does attract Whale Sharks and Manta Rays, and if you dive at either end of the leeward reefs, or on the windy sides of the islands, larger pelagics are common.

Aruba has sandy beaches and wrecks and Bonaire vies with Grand Cayman and Cozumel as the top Caribbean destination for American divers, while the much larger Curaçao has more varied topography. A substantial number of cetacean species frequent the area.

Whales and dolphins

Baleen whales include Blue, Bryde's, Fin, Humpback, Minke, and Sei. Bryde's Whale is the most sighted of the great whales, being most common in the summer and late autumn; and Humpbacks are relatively common in winter and spring.

The toothed whales to be enjoyed, include the following dolphins – Atlantic Bottlenose, Atlantic Spotted, Clymene, Pan-tropical Spotted, Rough-toothed, Fraser's, Risso's, Spinner and Striped.

The whales you may encounter include Blainville's Beaked, Cuvier's Beaked, Gervais' Beaked, False Killer, Killer, Pygmy Killer, Melon-headed, Pygmy Sperm, Shortfin Pilot, Dwarf Sperm and Sperm.

Of these, Shortfin Pilot Whales are seen throughout the year, and a lone Rough-toothed

Dolphin, which might have been an ex-captive specimen, befriended swimmers around Mangel Halto Reef, off Aruba, in the late 1990s.

Whale Sharks and sharks

Although not common, Whale Sharks do visit the leeward sides of the islands. One was even photographed on Aruba's Antilla Wreck.

Although there are plenty of predatory pelagic sharks on the windy sides of the islands, Scalloped Hammerheads are the main species observed by most divers, in areas such as at Punta Basora on the easternmost point of Aruba. Watamula and Playa Kalki at the western end of Curaçao give similar sightings. Lemon Sharks are often found in the inland bays and lagoons of Curaçao.

Turtles and Mantas

While Manta Rays are quite common it is the turtle that takes pride of place.

The people on Aruba, Bonaire and Curaçao take the protection of turtles nesting on their

beaches very seriously. The turtles that nest here from March to October are Green, Hawksbill, Loggerhead and Leatherback.

Ocean Sunfish

Other species that you may see include Ocean Sunfish, which are often seen in open water in this region.

Game fish are caught all year round in these waters, with sailfish, marlin, Wahoo and tuna being abundant offshore.

Opposite Shortfin Pilot Whales are actually members of the dolphin family; they are very sociable so it is rare to see them alone.

Below left The Atlantic Spotted Dolphin has a heavier body than its cousin, the Pan-tropical Spotted Dolphin and has a moderately long, chunky beak that is tipped with white.

Below right Hawksbill Turtles nest in the region and their migration routes are studied after attaching satellite transmitters while they are nesting.

CENTRAL CARIBBEAN
Close encounters with Whale Sharks

Lawson Wood

Nothing quite prepares you for that massive rush of excitement and adrenaline as you slip into the water over the side of a boat to face what can only be described as 'a monster of the deep'.

The visibility was poor that day, due to a massive plankton bloom that had spread across the entire Caribbean, following Hurricane Ivan.

Finding so much plankton, we should not have been surprised to find big plankton-eating creatures such as Whale Sharks and Manta Rays, but the experience still took us all by surprise.

The reef looked gloomy and dull, the light was filtered out by a vast, green-tinged plankton fog, that life-giving soup of the oceans. Then we saw the little fish, then bigger fish such as jacks, then hundreds of remoras; that's what gave this fish away. Whatever was following these little guys was big... very big!

Now, in among all this action and seemingly rushing towards us at a rate of knots were gigantic shark fins – preceded by a large, gaping mouth. Your reasoning tells you that this shark is a plankton eater and no threat, but your instinctive reaction tells you that this is most definitely a shark... and perhaps the scientists have got it wrong!

This encounter was with a Whale Shark, sighted off Placencia in Belize. Sensing that I was in front of its wide, blunt nose, the creature veered to one side like a submarine and looked me in the eye. I wonder what it thought of my clumsy, noisy attempts to keep up with the easy fluid motion of a creature that has evolved over millions of years, well before man came along to invade its territory.

Although the Whale Shark is the largest fish in the sea it feeds on the smallest of creatures. Very much a shark in shape, but reaching whale-like proportions, it has tough, spotted skin, gills and a vertical tail that it moves from side to side for propulsion. As the largest of the sharks it is also the largest fish and the largest cold-blooded animal in the world. By comparison, whales are warm-blooded, air-breathing mammals with a large tail that is horizontal in profile and is moved up and down for propulsion.

Often when they are approached too closely by snorkellers and divers, these sharks will stop in mid water and 'stand' on their tails. It is important not to grab a fin, as the creature will react as if being attacked from the rear. Believe me, a 20-tonne shark that puts on a burst of speed is formidable and can swat you aside like a piece of flotsam. The Shark Research Institute gave us specific instructions on how to interact with the Whale Shark without frightening or harming it... when it is still or moving slowly in the water, swim towards the head, to allow it to take a good look at you. And don't touch!

Whale Sharks are rarely seen any more than 500m (1640ft) from the shore as plankton levels are highest in these areas, and while this was a random encounter, they are seen fairly regularly off Belize from October to January. They are common off Aruba in the Netherlands Antilles, as well as Honduras, Cayman Islands and Mexico. More regular sightings are recorded off Trinidad, as this is one of the highest concentration areas for plankton in the Caribbean. This is due to the peculiar mix of freshwater that surges up from the Orinoco and further mixes with the sheltered waters of the Caribbean and cooler waters of the tropical western Atlantic. This creates a 'super-cell' of plankton, which attracts the largest volume feeders such as Whale Sharks and Manta Rays. From there, the sharks migrate past the island of Tobago from May to August before they pass into the main waters of the Caribbean.

Undoubtedly, what we experienced off Placencia, in Belize was a very special, almost humbling experience.

Right *Whale Sharks are generally always accompanied by juvenile fish such as pilot fish, cobia and remoras.*
Opposite *There is nothing like a really close encounter with the largest fish in the sea, the Whale Shark.*

THE CAYMANS

A celebration of turtles

Lawson Wood

Cayman Islands

Grand Cayman

Georgetown

East Point

Little Cayman

Cayman Brac

Spot Bay

Caribbean Sea

Cayman Trench

The Cayman Islands' flag, its official seal and currency all depict the turtle. The islands were originally called Las Tortugas by Christopher Columbus, and were named after the large numbers of turtles found on it and in its waters. And it was the turtle that brought sailors back to these enchanting islands. It was an important food supplement to the mariners' diet, because it could be kept alive – vital in those days before refrigeration.

Sadly, over the centuries the world's oceans have been depleted of many turtle species and all are on the international endangered species list. The Cayman Islands' turtle population was no exception, and suffered greatly, but fortunately however the tide has now turned for these animals and they are now bred for release.

The Turtle Farm on Grand Cayman Island was originally set up in 1968 as a private venture in order to breed turtles for release back into the wild.

In the very early stages, breeding stock and eggs had to be collected from the wild and it was agreed by the conservation authorities of several countries that eggs could be collected only from nests found below the tide line, where the eggs would have no chance of hatching. In time, collections came to be made from sources as far away as Surinam, Costa Rica and Ascension Island.

The farm moved to its present location in West Bay in 1971 and by 1978 had achieved its objective of having sufficient breeding stock to make it self-sufficient and financially viable. When the eggs are laid in the farm's enclosure, about 30 days after mating, they are collected and incubated. At 28°C (82°F) there will be an equal proportion of male and females hatched.

Any cooler and only males will emerge; any warmer and only females result. After hatching, the hatchlings are transferred to special tanks and fed on a specially formulated diet.

Some are selected from wild egg stock to enhance the breeding programme and perhaps the most interesting fact of all is that some 30,000 turtles have been released into the wild.

All of these animals have been tagged for scientific and recognition purposes. By means of constant monitoring it has been found that some of the turtles released in the Caymans have actually travelled as far afield as Mexico, Honduras, Cuba and Venezuela.

The turtle most favoured in the commercial breeding programme is the Green Turtle. There are also Hawksbill and Loggerhead Turtles at the farm, but one of their breeding successes is of the Kemp's Ridley Turtle.

Thanks to the careful release of the turtles, they can now be regularly seen on many dives, particularly in the protected waters of the Bloody Bay Marine Park along the northern shores of Little Cayman Island. Both Green and Hawksbill Turtles can be encountered on most dives. Seemingly unafraid of divers, they are quite passive and allow you to swim quite close to them. Not all of the turtles seen are tagged, however, which would indicate that there are some active nesting sites in the area that are helping to replenish the wild stock.

Above *Olive Ridley Turtles have been one of the great successes of the Cayman Turtle Farm.*

Top *Green Turtles with their much cleaner shell are more regularly found off Grand Cayman where they are released as part of a hatch-and-release programme at the Cayman Turtle Farm.*

Opposite *Hawksbill Turtles are commonly found among the shallow reefs and walls of Bloody Bay Wall on Little Cayman Island.*

BAHAMAS

For the thrill of shark-feeding

Lawson Wood

Only some 30-minutes flying time due east and south of Florida, the Bahamas group comprises some 700 islands, and 2500 small cays (pronounced keys) scattered over the tropical western Atlantic Ocean. Geologically, the Bahamas are the tips of a huge plateau that was once more than 90m (295ft) above sea level during the last Ice Age.

As the ice melted, the level of the seas rose, transforming the plateau into a vast submerged bank with waters just a few metres deep. This is a world-class diving area with excellent visibility, warm water, wrecks, caverns, blue holes and a super abundance of fish, stingrays, dolphins and sharks. Different areas have exciting features synonymous with their location. Moreover, in the Bahamas, they have capitalized on host interaction with a number of shark species.

Essentially these are spectator sports, where divers are positioned in a semicircle and wait as large groups of sharks come in and take bait from the experienced shark wranglers. The visiting species are usually Caribbean Reef Sharks but several pelagic species also arrive to check out the cause of the commotion.

There is a daily shark-feeding programme at Shark Junction, just a 10-minute boat ride from the dock. A detailed briefing is given before each trip and divers are made aware of the risks involved with hand-feeding large wild animals.

On first entering the water, you assemble in front of an old recompression chamber that was sunk as a dive site, and the shark-feeder arrives with a container full of fish. Snappers, groupers, Horse-eye Jacks, amberjacks, stingrays, and sharks soon surround him. Safety divers position themselves at the edges of the group and the shark-feeder dressed in a chain-mail suit controls the action, with the bulk of the bait being kept in an enclosed PVC tube.

After several years of acclimatisation, the sharks now rush in and out of the feeding area, taking the bait from the feeder's hand; in some cases, he will stroke the sharks, particularly the larger females. These sharks not only react to feeding, they also love the tactile sensation and come well within arm's reach of the spectators, who, unlike the feeder, are requested to resist the temptation to touch the sharks.

Long Island was the first area to have shark-feeding over 20 years ago and the method has remained largely unchanged throughout that time. A similar dive has been organized on Shark Reef. It is conducted in a frenzy with – somewhat disconcertingly – sharks already circling beneath you as you enter the water from the dive boat; from here on in, the bucket of

Right *The shark-feeding session out at the Runway is a great spectator sport with superb chances of photographing large sharks in a natural reef environment.*
Opposite *The Walkers Cay shark-feed around the frozen 'chumsickle' is one of the best opportunities to photograph large numbers of different species of sharks, all at the same time.*

fish provided by the feeder is quickly devoured amid a torrent of action that can only be described as 'high-voltage'.

On Walkers Cay in the Abacos, the operators have developed a similar ritualized feed, but here the shark frenzy attracts literally hundreds of sharks that attack a large barrel of frozen bait known locally as a 'chumsickle'. This is lowered among a group of nervous and awe-struck divers. Although the predominant encounter is with Caribbean Reef Sharks, quite often Scalloped Hammerheads will vie with Shortfin Mako, Lemon, Bull, Nurse and Tiger sharks for space and scraps. Be warned: this is not for the faint-hearted or those with a nervous disposition.

However, it is actually one of the safest shark encounters, as the human feeder has been removed from the equation, thus concentrating the sharks' attention on the frozen bait.

It is curiously thrilling to enter the shark-feeding arena and watch the pecking order develop over which shark gets to eat next.

Once the bait has been devoured, divers can look for the teeth dislodged during the feeding. Walkers Cay used to be one of the few locations in the world where you could snorkel with Bull Sharks in the shallow waters but this was banned after a researcher got silly in front of a film team and was bitten.

Possibly the greatest variety of shark encounters is to be found south of Nassau, the capital of the Bahamas, on New Providence Island. Here at Stuart Cove's Dive South Ocean, there is controlled feeding, but the excitement is particularly high when you first

(20ft) in diameter, has created its own open-ocean ecosystem; the lower surface is covered by a film of algae, which attracts small fish. Other species such as jacks and triggerfish seek shelter under the buoy and these in turn attract the larger and more efficient predators – sharks.

After the buoy was first moored, sports and commercial fishermen soon discovered how favourable the area had become and would catch the sharks, remove their fins and jaw and cast the carcass into the depths. It was by chance that Stuart saw the potential for one of the most exhilarating diving experiences in the world.

That first dive under the buoy so captured his imagination that he returned time after time, growing more despondent when he saw the newly resident shark population being depleted almost daily. Stuart said: 'They were being drastically reduced in number and at one point, they were completely fished out. Fortunately the location of the buoy is such that sharks will continue to be attracted by the activity that is created around it.'

After many discussions with commercial and sport-fishing organizations in the Bahamas, as well as individual sport-fishermen, shark experts and conservation groups, an agreement was finally reached that there would be no long line fishing around the buoy and that any sharks caught by sports-fishermen would be released.

Another problem was then encountered, namely that the Silky Sharks now had hooks, barbs and lures protruding from their jaws. Obviously it is uncomfortable and in some cases a real hindrance to feeding. Many had broken off during the time they were briefly hooked by the fishermen, other hooks had line and lure attached where they had been cut free, and some of the hooks were rusty. So Stuart decided they should be removed. But how?

He had learned of a harmless way to immobilize the sharks. The technique induces what is called 'torpid immobility' and involves grabbing hold of the tip of the shark's tail and

enter the water as part of a two-tank dive to the Shark Wall and Runway. Stuart Cove offers three distinct types of shark dive.

At Shark Wall, divers enter the water on the lip of the ocean trench that drops 1830m (6000ft). On the second dive, the shark-feeder leads you a little way in from the lip of the wall into a wide, sandy, natural amphitheatre. The sharks are fed using a pole-spear and you can quickly recognize the routes they take. If you position yourself in one of these passes, you can have a face-to-face encounter with the sharks as they enter and leave the arena.

The third type of encounter is much freer and therefore more unpredictable... it's an encounter with Silky Sharks. This species is found in the offshore waters of The Tongue of the Ocean, a trench, 1830m (6000ft) deep, that bisects the Bahamas between New Providence Island and Andros Island. This is seen more as a pure encounter between man and shark, in the blue of the ocean.

When Stuart Cove told me that he and his cousin Graham were going out to the naval buoy to capture Silky Sharks by hand and remove fish-hooks from their mouths, I had to go along! Forty minutes after leaving the dock at Dive South Ocean, we reached the massive United States Naval Buoy that is used to track their submarines. The buoy, itself some 6m bending it, turning the shark on to its back; the creature immediately becomes dull, unresponsive and almost catatonic for between 30 and 90 seconds. He was told that this would be enough time to remove the hook and then release the animal, with relatively little risk to the catcher. The problem was how to catch the shark in the first place?

Easy enough, just bait the water, attract the sharks to feed in front of you and when one gets close enough, grab it by the tail! Surprisingly, the scheme worked.

Stuart and Graham were able to bait the sharks, bringing them closer and closer until they could be gripped by the tail and 'torpid immobility' induced. Stuart held the shark by the tail and supported the rest of its body while Graham removed the offending hook. The shark was immediately released and swam off with no side effects whatsoever.

Says Stuart: 'The smaller Silky Sharks are more of a challenge as they're much faster and you only have a short time to carry out the manoeuvre. Another problem is that after you manage to handle two or three, the rest get spooked and it may be several hours before they will again come close, even when there is bait in the water'. I asked Stuart if any other sharks appeared while this was going on.

'Yes,' he said, 'We have had Tiger Sharks, Mako and Caribbean Reef Sharks. Once we even had a hammerhead swim right between us, just checking out what was going on.'

The United States Naval Buoy in the Bahamas has got to be one of the most exciting open-water diving locations in the world. Where else can you swim over an ocean trench 1830m (6000ft) deep, and catch Silky Sharks by the tail? Taken together, the Bahamas shark dives offer perhaps the greatest variety of shark encounters available in the world today.

These are truly honest-to-goodness, really exciting adventures in what many divers believe is now the shark capital of the world.

Above *While the Caribbean Reef Shark is not pelagic, witnessing an adrenalin-charged feed by divers in chain-mail suits is exhilarating.*

Opposite top *Blacktip Sharks are the other most commonly seen species during the Caribbean shark-feeding sessions.*

Opposite bottom *Nurse Sharks, although fairly docile, can become quite aggressive during the shark-feeding sessions and care should be taken.*

AZORES
Where wandering Ocean Sunfish visit

Stephen Wong and Takako Uno

ATLANTIC OCEAN

São Jorge — Graciosa
Flores
Faial — Pico — Terceira
São Miguel
Santa Maria

Azores (Portugal)

Madeira (Portugal)

The Azores (Açôres) is a group of nine volcanic islands in the Atlantic, about 1450km (900 miles) from Portugal and 3700km (2300 miles) from North America.

The islands' underwater seascape is very similar to its landscape, with the dark lava of the ocean floor forming the backdrop. However, though diving here may seem to be less colourful than that found in the Indo-Pacific, its sea life is some of the most interesting... you'll find big game fish and migratory cetaceans in the waters off the Azores, and also the wandering Ocean Sunfish.

We had been after sperm whales one morning off the western end of Pico Island. I had been in the water at least 15 times but apart from whale waste and dead skin hadn't seen a single specimen. But, as always, as soon as we were back on the inflatable, the whales would reappear, regroup and lazily hang out at the surface.

Then, suddenly, our radio came to life... 'Steve! We have a sunfish here! Get over here before it disappears.' It was Ralf Kiefner, calling us from the other boat, some distance away.

In an instant I grabbed the microphone and established where they were. It turned out it would take 40 minutes to get there. I felt like an ant on a hot wok! In 40 minutes the sunfish would have gone; it was definitely a wild goose chase! Still, our skipper Michael opened the throttles and we were off.

Suddenly, barely into the journey, we saw a pod of large dolphins on the horizon.

'Pseudorcas!' yelled Michael.

This created a dilemma. We had never seen a False Killer Whale and this was a golden opportunity. Thinking that I had the perfect solution, I suggested we go to the sunfish first, and then return for the whales.

Michael disagreed. 'We won't be able to return to these whales... they're travelling very fast – and in the opposite direction.'

We were in a quandary.

Finally, we decided to view the whales. Almost immediately, a large adult turned towards us, its gleaming white teeth clearly visible – and we were back in the inflatable in seconds! Michael opened the throttles again, and soon we saw Ralf's boat; my heart lightened when I saw that he was still in the water.

The sunfish had waited for us after all!

I was out of the boat before it stopped. Without signalling to Ralf, who was filming, I butted in as I was so afraid that the fish would disappear. Ralf had already had the fish for two hours. Now the Chinese-Japanese couple would claim their share!

The Ocean Sunfish's scientific name *Mola mola* comes from the Latin term '*mola*', meaning millstone, which this creature resembles... in a

Right *The Ocean Sunfish is a cartoon-like character, here accompanied by pilot fish.*

Opposite *An Ocean Sunfish at the surface ignores the close attendance of a swimmer.*

way. It's very unusual – it seems to have forgotten its tail! A relative of the pufferfish it's shaped like a huge oblong dining plate, with small pectoral fins, a single gill flap on each side, very large cartoon-character-like eyes and a small mouth.

The tail, such as it is, is used as a rudder, and is one of the shortest in the fish kingdom. The strangest thing is the way that the sunfish swims: it propels itself clumsily and slowly through the water by flapping its dorsal and ventral fins.

These fish spend most of their time in the depths- down to 1000 m (3000ft), but usually 300m (1000ft) – where they feed on their favourite food, jellyfish and salps. Occasionally, however, they rise to the surface to bask and be cleaned by seabirds and small fish.

The sunfish can grow to 4m (13ft) and weigh up to 2000kg (4400lb), which makes it the world's largest bony fish.

However, its lack of tail and method of swimming make it easy prey for most predators; but it does have two main defences – its foul taste and its thick skin: a 1.7m (6ft) specimen can have skin 15cm (6in) thick. However, even this is not a completely effective deterrent, and in Californian waters sunfish are mauled and eaten

by sea lions. In addition, their skin doesn't have scales, which makes it more susceptible to attacks by parasites, and lesions.

Well, there were no sea lions here, and this sunfish seemed happy, lying on its side on the surface of a flat sea with blue sky above (it is thought that basking to absorb solar energy might speed up the fish's digestion). So there it

lay, its mouth opening and closing, the lips pursed as if blowing smoke rings – or offering indiscriminate kisses to all and sundry.

After a while, it returned to its normal upright position and started to circle me. As we became familiar with each other, it paused and tilted its head. Suddenly I remembered as a TV documentary flashed through my mind:

Hey, it's inviting me to clean its body! The tall dorsal fin flapped gently, seeming to say, 'Come on, give me a rub!'

Mesmerized, I closed in, but suddenly noticed that it had a patch of dying skin near to its tail. Observing the giant fish from barely a metre (40in), I could see hundreds of parasites. But not only did the grotesque creatures deter

Above A Great Sperm Whale at the surface; an adult can eat up to a tonne of squid in a day.
Left Great Sperm Whales socializing.
Opposite An Ocean Sunfish at the surface with its attendant cleaner fish.

me, but also the notion of touching a wild animal stopped me from reaching out.

Then, as if by arrangement, a flashing shoal of sardines arrived and became masseurs. As the sun's rays shimmered through the water, it created a curtain of light as these small fish dashed in and out, eagerly tending the sunfish.

It was a perfect symbiotic relationship as the small fish, as if choreographed by the gentle giant's long, slowly swaying fins, busily danced to the music of a silent sea. For the next 45 minutes, the sunfish remained with us and followed us about like a puppy. Its friendliness surprised even Michael, a seasoned skipper, and he joined us in the water. But Ralf had missed out – he was long gone!

We stayed in as long we could, enjoying this unique experience until the penetrating cold of the water forced us back on board. But the sunfish still stayed with us. Eventually, when leaving, we slapped the water to make the fish move away so that it would be safe from our propellors.

As we reluctantly departed, we glanced back and saw that the creature was basking again. A fin waved to us, almost in a lazy farewell, before the great fish disappeared below the surface to continue on its lonely journey through the sea.

THE UNITED KINGDOM

Home to an astounding range of pelagics

Jack Jackson

The temperate waters of the UK are often murky but they have plenty of interesting fish and marine mammals including pelagic species. Fin, Minke and pilot whales and other dolphins and porpoises, various sharks and marine turtles are all found in British waters.

To the west the warm Gulf Stream gives the UK a warmer climate than would otherwise be the case and brings some surprising visitors including Ocean Sunfish and marine turtles. The whole western half of the UK sees Basking Sharks in spring and summer. So while many divers tend to think first of the tropics and other warmer waters when considering their next dive excursion, don't rule the UK out of the equation.

Whales and dolphins

The seas around Britain and Ireland are among the richest in Europe for whales and dolphins. Some are resident but most are only passing through and sightings may be rare.

However, when a sighting is made, its rarity value makes it even more enjoyable and rewarding. The greatest chances of spotting a range of these animals are on whale-watching boat trips in Scottish waters.

The baleen whales include the following:

Blue Whales – probably the largest animals that have ever lived, these ocean giants occur regularly in small numbers in winter, with peak sightings in November and December.

Fin Whales – the most common whales to the west of Scotland, are present year-round, with a lull in activity from May to July.

Humpback Whales – have only been detected acoustically between mid-November and March, but have been sighted at other times of the year.

Minke Whales – the most common whale seen in UK waters.

The toothed whales include the following:

Atlantic White-sided Dolphins – seen from June to November along the continental shelf slope west of the Atlantic coast of Ireland and Scotland, and north of Shetland and Orkney.

Beluga Whales – rare, but they may be seen off Shetland.

Bottlenose Dolphins – many inshore Bottlenose Dolphins are resident in one area year-round, such as those in Scotland's Moray Firth so viewing opportunities in these areas may be considered to be good.

Common Dolphins – some are resident while other populations migrate seasonally.

Cuvier's Beaked Whales – recorded from the southwest approaches to the English Channel, Western Ireland and the Western Isles of Scotland.

Harbour Porpoises – this is the only porpoise in European waters. The majority of sightings occur within 10km (6 miles) of land. Bottle-nose Dolphins around British coasts are killing Harbour Porpoises, possibly due to competition for food.

Killer whales – often occur in UK waters, sometimes hunting Basking Sharks. They are most common in northern and western Scotland. They are found throughout the year, but come inshore between May and October.

Longfin Pilot Whales – seasonally enter coastal areas of the Faeroe Islands, northern Scotland, western Ireland and the approach to the southwest English Channel. They occur in the northern UK from June–September and then further south from November–January.

Northern Bottlenose Whales – found in small numbers around the Northern and Western Isles of Scotland, in the northern North Sea and along the west of Ireland from April–September.

Risso's Dolphins – seen in the western part of the English Channel, the Irish Sea, off the

Left *Beluga Whales are rare but sometimes seen off Shetland.*

Above left *Longfin Pilot Whales are quite common seasonally; their body-shape varies considerably with age and sex.*

Opposite *Basking Sharks swim near the surface with their mouths wide open, sieving the plankton.*

coast of Dyfed in Wales, and the west coast of Scotland, such as the Isle of Mull. They usually stay in warm waters, but they have been seen in cooler waters during the summer.

Sowerby's Beaked Whales – these have been seen south to the English Channel, but they are mainly encountered offshore, north and west of the UK.

Sperm whales – occur along the edge of the continental shelf north and west of the UK from July-December. They are usually either adult or adolescent males, which have migrated from subtropical and tropical breeding areas.

Striped Dolphins – rare in UK waters and mainly seen to the southwest.

True's Beaked Whales – rare but they are recorded west of the Outer Hebrides, and off the west coasts of Ireland, and England; they're possibly associated with the Gulf Stream.

Whitebeak Dolphins – live in northern oceans up to the edge of the pack ice but are rarely seen south of the English Channel.

Sharks in UK waters

Many species of sharks have been recorded in UK waters, particularly those to the west, but the larger predatory pelagic sharks are offshore and rarely encountered by divers. Surprisingly, there is a hammerhead shark that can live in relatively cold water from the western coast of Ireland and southern UK in the summer.

Sharks found in UK waters include Blue, Bluntnose Sixgill, Greenland, Smooth Hammerhead, Shortfin Mako, Porbeagle, Bigeye Thresher and Common Thresher.

For snorkellers, the main sharks of interest are Basking Sharks, the second largest fish in the world. They feed on plankton so you can snorkel

with them when they are on the surface but you must put their wellbeing first. While helping a film crew to film Basking Sharks in bright, flat-calm conditions around the Isle of Arran, we would not encounter any Basking Sharks in the mornings but would see up to 50 each afternoon when they followed the plankton to the surface.

There are three hotspots for sightings. These are southwest England, the Isle of Man and Scotland's Firth of Clyde.

The sharks are first seen on the surface off southwest England in February with peak sightings in May and again in July. Then off the Isle of Man with peak sightings in June, and off Scotland with peak sightings in August, there are also good numbers seen here in September.

Records also show a north-south movement from the Isle of Man to southwest England. Sometimes large shoals of over 100 occur and even as many as 500 were reported off Cornwall's Lizard Point in 1998.

Marine turtles

Five of the world's seven species of marine turtles have been seen in UK waters. These are the Green, Hawksbill, Kemp's Ridley, Leatherback and Loggerhead. However, only Leatherbacks are considered to be regular and intentional visitors.

Although nesting on tropical beaches, Leatherbacks feed mainly on jellyfish in tropical, sub-tropical and temperate waters. With some control over their body temperature, they can remain active and feed in cooler waters. Research has shown that Leatherbacks do not stay long in tropical waters but spend most of their time in food-rich northern waters.

In fact adult Leatherbacks are so common in UK waters in late summer and autumn that some people would like them to be re-classified as a UK species, which only visits the Caribbean to breed.

The largest specimen ever recorded was found washed up at Harlech, Wales in 1988.

It was truly massive, weighed 916kg (2020lb) and was 2.91m (9.55ft) long.

Other marine turtles that are encountered in the UK are likely to be juvenile or sub-adult Loggerhead and Kemp's Ridley Turtles. Sightings of Green and Hawksbill Turtles are rare, however. Unlike Leatherbacks, the other marine turtles will have been transported from warmer climes by currents and storms. These animals are usually suffering from the cold and in poor health. If you come across such a turtle, contact the Marine Conservation Society or the nearest public aquarium as quick action can save its life.

Ocean Sunfish

Mola mola, those strangely shaped but nevertheless fascinating denizens of the deep, are quite commonly recorded all along the south and west of the UK and all around Scotland, feeding on organisms from jellyfish to algae. They are thought to have been carried on ocean currents, such as the North Atlantic Drift – which is a continuation of the Gulf Stream – into UK waters. In the past, Arran Islanders hunted them with harpoons. As many as 12 have been seen together off the Scilly Isles.

So, despite the fact that the waters of the UK might lack the many brightly-coloured reef-dwellers and the corals of warmer waters, there is a great deal to see and experience, especially the immense Basking Sharks.

SOUTH AFRICA, CAPE SHARKS

The raw power of the sharks of the Cape

Chris and Monique Fallows

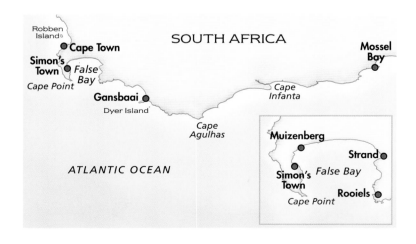

South Africa's southern Cape and southwest coast is blessed with rich shark fauna that contains not only the big glamorous species but also many endemic species unique to the area. Here, however, we will deal with two very different forms of shark encounters.

The first part of this chapter deals with Great White Sharks, where the chosen form of diving is within a cage close inshore and around seal colonies. The second part deals with true pelagic diving with other pelagic sharks, far offshore in water that is typically over 1000m (3280ft) deep.

Successful commercial Great White cage-diving began in South Africa in 1991–2 off Dyer Island, Gansbaai, about 180km (110 miles) east of Cape Town. Mossel Bay, 400km (248 miles) from Cape Town then followed suit, as did Simon's Town, False Bay, in 1996. Simon's Town is the closest at just 30km (19 miles) from the city centre.

All three sites offer different opportunities and have their own pros and cons. The vessels used are usually powerboats, with the exception of Mossel Bay where a motorized sailing catamaran is the vessel of choice. Passenger group sizes vary from six in False Bay to upwards of 30 in Gansbaai and vessels accordingly cater for the needs of the different markets.

All Great White Shark dives are made from cages. However, some operators allow snorkelling within the cage while others insist on scuba and qualified divers only.

Mossel Bay is home to a large but seasonal population of Great Whites that swim very close to shore and around a 6000-strong seal colony. Mossel Bay shark activity can be very intense and during the summer months many hammerheads can be seen cruising along on the surface while you are en route to the day's Great White encounter.

Visibility here can be the best of the three localities, especially when the warm Agulhas Current sweeps into the bay, bringing warm blue water. Unlike Dyer and Seal Islands, however, there is no channel and so all diving is done either close to the island or off the coast close to nearby river mouths.

For me the greatest advantage of Mossel Bay is the fact that there is only one operator, who runs a large sailing catamaran, so you do not need to worry about who will see the sharks. If they are there, you will.

You may also have the chance to see Great Whites breach and hunt seals. Both experiences

are rare, but they are spectacular – and once you have seen them, you will never forget them.

Dyer Island, 9km (6 miles) off the fishing village of Gansbaai, is the most famous of the three localities due to the large number of operators offering cage-diving. This spectacular island is home to many species of birds, which gather in their thousands. Adjacent to Dyer Island, Geyser Rock contains upwards of 50,000 Cape Fur Seals. Shark Alley lies between the two, a shallow channel around 5m (16ft) deep, where most of the cage-diving takes place from April–October.

Usually the best time to see intense shark activity is just before or after a cold front has

passed, but make sure that you take your sea-sickness remedies along as Dyer Island is exposed to the Cape's famous winter seas.

The water inside the channel can be clear with occasional days having visibility of 15m (50ft) or more and one of the unique characteristics of the channel is that you can usually see the bottom. Sharks can therefore be seen at any depth as they cruise the channel hunting for stray seals.

During the remainder of the year, i.e. the late spring and summer months, the operators move away from the island and closer to shore as the Great Whites now hunt and interact in these regions. Visibility is seldom as good as

Right *A large female Silvertip Shark casually observes divers clamouring for a better look at her.*

Opposite *A 4m (13ft) Great White explodes from the water showing all the attributes that make it one of the ocean's greatest predators.*

near the island, nor is the action usually as intense. Sharks are seen on most days, however.

The disadvantage of Dyer Island for Great White diving is the intense competition. With eight operators and visiting scientists, everyone is compelled to work in close proximity for a limited resource and therefore it can become somewhat crowded.

However, if you are into thrills and don't mind the crowds this would be my first choice as a cage-diving venue in South Africa as bookings and shark sightings seldom pose a problem.

Close to Cape Town, Seal Island, in False Bay, is home to 60,000 seals and a variety of seabirds and the island itself lies protected

deep within the bay. There are three operators working here, although on many days only one or two boats will be in the area.

The island is unique as it offers unsurpassed opportunities to see Great Whites hunting seals and on many days during the winter months you may see multiple hunts. It is also the area world famous for breaching Great Whites and these awesome displays of power and aerial hunting prowess are unforgettable. Cage-diving is offered at Seal Island and the area can sometimes have spectacular visibility similar to that at Dyer Island. The focus here is on natural viewing from the boat and anyone who would like to concentrate

on multiple aspects of Great White Shark behaviour and not just cage-diving is certain find this the best venue.

False Bay has a short but very intense season starting at the end of April and usually finishing in late September. The island has the advantage of being sheltered from the winter storms, and when the other localities are blown out Seal Island is often calm and workable. However, during the summer months of November–February, shark activity is typically low. This, coupled with the south-easterly winds, means it is a venue where we would recommend contacting the operators first, to check on recent sightings and weather

forecasts, before making a booking. You do, however, have the advantage of seeing the spectacular Cape Point Nature Reserve and Boulders African Penguin colony should your day be blown out, so all is not lost.

All sites are seasonal and have ebbs and flows in sightings. So, with this in mind, we would recommend you contact your operator of choice before booking. Try to plan at least two days for this activity as weather plays a large part in whether trips can be offered. The good news is that all areas offer some great alternative activities to suit all tastes should you need to fill your time while the wind blows itself out.

It is also important to note that the operators use chumming to various degrees to attract sharks. Chum is usually a mixture of ground-up fish, similar to that used by commercial fishermen to entice fish into feeding close to their boats. Some operators unfortunately do use shark livers mixed with the fish and this practice threatens those species killed for their livers. Bait, usually in the form of fish-heads, is placed in the water to keep the sharks interested when close to the boat.

Operators do not purposely feed sharks and in most cases every effort is made to avoid feeding them. We would recommend being environmentally sensitive in your choice of operator as great efforts are made by many to do things the right way and to educate guests on the importance and beauty of these magnificent animals.

Right *Some of the 64,000 Cape Fur Seals that live on Seal Island frolic in its waters during the heat of day.*

Above right *A large Great White Shark breaches as the sun rises in False Bay, showing the beautiful colouring of this massive animal.*

Opposite *A Great White misses a young Cape Fur Seal in this first dramatic lunge, leaving observers spellbound by the David and Goliath battles to be seen at Seal Island.*

Pelagic shark diving off Cape Point

The dictionary definition of pelagic is as follows: 'pertaining to the open ocean away from the sea bottom'. So why in the world would anyone want to go out where land cannot be seen, other people are a rarity, and the water can be over 1000m (3280ft) deep?

The answer lies in all of these things, but is coupled to the fact that for some of the ocean's most spectacular creatures this blue, clear, warm domain is home. So it's easy to see why, for some of us, the allure of the deep is simply over-whelming. However, occasionally it can also be a very hostile environment with massive storms and mountainous seas.

Cape Point, South Africa, is 34° S, 18° E and home to some of the greatest concentrations and diversity of species found anywhere. Here, the great ocean currents mix and the mosaic of currents, water temperature and upwelling creates the perfect environment for a multitude of the pelagic world's best creatures.

Our search is targeted towards the sharks, namely the sinuous Blue Sharks, which average 1.5m (5ft) in length but have been known to reach a length of 3.8m (12ft) and the beauti-fully streamlined Mako Sharks, which average 1.6m (5ft), but on rare occasions reach just over 4m (13ft). To find these sharks we look for a variety of sea-conditions, the presence of fish and anything else that may attract these open ocean nomads.

Once we have selected a site, usually one about 40–65km (23–40 miles) offshore,

Left *Yellowfin Tuna of up to 100kg are often seen on pelagic dives; truly a beautiful sight.*
Above left *The Shortfin Mako Shark is one of the ocean's fastest fish, and one of the most streamlined.*
Opposite *A Great White swims up close to the camera, dominating boat and photographer alike.*

we lower our low-frequency sound equipment into the water and with the lure of a fresh fish slick, we send out our calling card to these cobalt-blue hunters. While we wait for them to arrive we drift along at the will of the currents and winds.

During our wait we also see many species of albatross and a multitude of other pelagic birds that make this one of the best spots in the world to see open ocean birds. We commonly see various cetacean species as well, and also often attract huge Yellowfin and Longfin Tuna, both spectacular companions on a dive. But, it's the sharks we've come to see, and there's

pandemonium when we spot the first dorsal fin. People grab cameras and gasp in amazement at the beauty of these magnificent animals. In most cases there is an overpowering urge to get into the water with them.

Our modus operandi is to free dive with the sharks very close to the boat. No cages nor chain-mail suits are used because, like most sharks, they are not openly aggressive unless provoked. The group size is limited to six guests to ensure a personal experience.

Each guest is equipped with a plastic prodding-pole to gently fend off any over-curious shark should the need arise. However,

we often find that after a short period of acclimatization, most guests want the sharks to come closer to get a better view of their grace and beauty. No more than two guests are ever in the water at any time and are always accompanied by one of us.

Naturally, the sharks come and go as they please and the thrill of never knowing what will turn up next always adds to the adventure.

However, the success rate in seeing sharks is at 90 per cent and on virtually all trips something exciting will be seen.

For anyone with a true love of nature and a taste for adventure this is a trip not to be missed.

Above *A Bottlenose Dolphin interacts with a snorkeller, off Nuweiba, Egypt. It was here that a female Spotted Dolphin named Olin befriended a deaf, mute Bedouin.*

Red Sea & Indian Ocean

THE RED SEA

Waters with a wealth of pelagic species

Jack Jackson

Despite being a narrow stretch of water with only a small outlet to the Indian Ocean, the Red Sea has many pelagic species. A few come in from the Mediterranean via the Suez Canal but most enter via the Arabian Sea and Gulf of Aden.

While cruising on a dive boat from Suakin, south of Port Sudan, we would constantly see whales blowing at the surface but unfortunately we could never get near enough to identify them. A number have been recorded, however. Whale Sharks are relatively common, especially at Djibouti, and have

been well recorded by divers all the way north to the head of the Gulf of Aqaba. Dolphins are everywhere, either in relatively fixed areas where they can reach shelter in bad weather, or when migrating. Some in Sudanese, Egyptian, Israeli and Jordanian waters have become used to encounters with divers. In fact, some of those in Egyptian waters now need protection, because non-diving operators were bringing too many snorkellers to the parts of reefs that the dolphins inhabit. The larger, pelagic sharks are found anywhere that they can escape to deep water when water temperatures get too warm or there are too many divers around. However, even heavily dived reefs such as those at Sharm el Sheikh still have the shark populations that made them famous in the 1970s, but they are now mostly found in deep water, or at night.

Manta Rays can also be found throughout the Red Sea and there are some reefs where encounters are almost guaranteed if divers remain quiet or, better still, snorkel. There are also marine turtles to be seen everywhere. Green, Hawksbill, Loggerhead, Olive Ridley and, occasionally, Leatherback Turtles, are even

Opposite *Some lone dolphins actively seek out human company.*
Below *In some areas Bryde's Whales will feed predominantly on krill but in other areas they prefer small shoaling fish.*

found on wrecks where those that feed on sponges have good pickings. Turtles need quiet beaches for egg-laying and many in the north are being developed for tourism. However, there are still some countries with low populations and some sandy islands that the turtles use.

Large tuna are often seen on dives, flashing past 20m (66ft) away, but game fish like sailfish and marlin are mostly seen jumping clear of the water at a distance of 100m (328ft) or more. There is no organized game-fishing industry but expatriates and wealthy Egyptians, Saudi Arabians and Sudanese do go out for these on a Friday if the weather is good.

Whales and dolphins

The Arabian Sea contains so many species of whales and dolphins that whale-watching trips have been proposed. Whale species that have been spotted just 3–4km (2–3 miles) off Muscat include Bryde's, Humpback, sperm

and False Killer Whales. A lone Blue Whale was seen in the 1800s and another one in 1996. The dolphins to be seen include Risso's, Bottlenose, Spinner and Common.

Most of these species, and Sei Whales, Killer Whales, Indo-Pacific Hump-backed dolphins, Pan-tropical Spotted Dolphins, Shortfin Pilot Whales, Spinner and Striped Dolphins find their way into the Red Sea.

Dolphins are extremely common. Some move around in large pods while remaining within an hour of sheltered lagoons to which they can retreat in bad weather. Others migrate long distances and some, such as Bottlenose Dolphins, constantly circle reefs like Sanganeb and Sha'b Rumi in pods of 3–10.

Bottlenose Dolphins are attracted to drifting boats such as those covering divers on drift-dives. Off the East Face of Sanganeb, I have had large Bottlenose Dolphins leap out of the water within metres of the boat and reach the

height of my flying-bridge – 4m (13ft). West of Sanganeb I have seen huge shoals of migrating pilot whales feeding on shoals of tuna.

In Sudan, at Sanganeb, there is a permanent mixture of Common and Bottlenose Dolphins that venture as far as Sha'b Rumi during the day and rest overnight or in bad weather in the outer lagoon at Sanganeb. These dolphins are completely at ease with live-aboard dive boats anchoring in this lagoon. In fact at night they often rest on the surface beside these boats. I am sure that similar pods exist wherever there are similar sheltered lagoons.

I have occasionally seen Risso's Dolphins as well. I saw two near the West Face of Sanganeb, and seven between Jackson Reef and Laguna north of Tiran Island in Egypt, and others further north in the Gulf of Aqaba. With their rounded snouts and pale bodies, these shy giants resemble Beluga Whales. They tend to prefer offshore habitats in warm temperate and tropical waters.

As well as organized dolphin encounters with ex-dolphinarium animals off Eilat there are some dolphins that have sought human company in the past. For instance, off Nuweiba in the Egyptian part of the Gulf of Aqaba, a female Spotted Dolphin named Olin befriended a deaf, mute Bedouin.

Other encounters include the Spinner Dolphins at Sha'b Samadai (Dolphin House Reef) in southern Egypt. There, however, the numbers of divers and snorkellers have had to be limited and a fee levied to protect the dolphins from harassment.

Whale Sharks

The Republic of Djibouti, between Eritrea, Ethiopia and Somalia, has a marine life that results from the mixing of the waters of the Red Sea and the Indian Ocean.

A copious amount of plankton attracts mantas and migrating Whale Sharks, mostly juveniles 5–7m (16–22ft), between October and the end of January. Although the visibility will obviously be poor, these sharks and mantas are found along the Gulf of Tadjourah, in the Bay of Arta, and Goubhet El Kharab.

Goubhet El Kharab, which is connected by a narrow channel to the Gulf of Tadjourah, is called the Devil's Cauldron by the locals. It is the start of the Great Rift Valley and the junction between the African and Arabian continental plates. The Whale Sharks found further north, including in the Gulf of Aqaba, are mostly juveniles but they still look remarkably large.

Sharks

Sharks are still very common in the Red Sea, and they are still routinely fished off Yemen. Dried shark meat travels well in the desert so the creatures are caught for food and their fins are just a by-product.

Despite claims by Hans Hass, I have never seen a Great White Shark in the Red Sea but there are many other species, especially on offshore reefs. Even in the far north, Oceanic Whitetip Sharks and Tiger Sharks follow pods of dolphins in open water – so snorkelling in open water with dolphins is not advisable.

Scalloped Hammerheads and Oceanic Whitetips are found at all offshore reefs in Egypt and Sudan though the Scalloped Hammerheads are more likely to be seen because they like to shoal. Thresher Sharks are seen over deep water such as at Dædalus Reef, whereas Tiger Sharks are scavengers and so they are often found at the entrance to ports. They tend to stay deep during the day and come into shallow water at night.

In May 1980, Hans Hass experimented by leaving hooked meat attached to floating oil drums outside Port Sudan overnight and caught several large Tiger Sharks. I have

Left *A head-on view of the largest fish in the sea.*
Opposite top *Tiger Sharks are scavengers, they will eat almost anything including rubbish near harbours.*
Opposite bottom *Scalloped Hammerhead Sharks are often seen in large shoals.*

is patrolled by several species of sharks around 8:00. One morning I was escorting a novice diver on his first relatively deep dive so I was not carrying a camera and true to Sod's Law, we had eight, 1m (40in) juvenile Scalloped Hammerhead Sharks swimming around us and between our legs for five minutes.

The hammerhead shoal off the South Point of Sha'b Rumi is only about 30 strong and they remain in deep water. The same tends to apply at the southern end of Elphinstone Reef in Egypt, although I was once very lucky there when other divers spooked three sharks into swimming over my head and I was able to get a good photograph.

Scalloped Hammerheads tend to range in length from about 2–4m (6.5–13ft), but the larger Great Hammerheads can reach 6m (20ft) with a very large, pointed first dorsal fin. They tend to be solitary and migratory, heading for cooler water during the summer months.

The best reefs to see the larger Great Hammerheads are St John's, and both Scalloped and Great Hammerheads are seen at Brothers Islands and Dædalus Reef in Egypt.

Other areas to see shoals of Scalloped Hammerheads are all offshore reefs in Sudan, and the north side of Jackson Reef, Sha'b Sharm, the north plateau Abu Kafan, Fury Shoal, Sataya Reef and Habili Reefs in Egypt.

Silky Sharks can get too belligerent and have scared many divers out of the water at Sha'b Rumi. I was once running a shark-feed at the Southwest Point of Sanganeb when all of the sharks disappeared as a battle-torn male Silky came in. He harassed each of the eight divers in turn before grabbing the bait and we took this opportunity to leave the water. Occasionally you get Silvertips at Sanganeb but they are very common off the South Point of Sha'b Rumi.

Much larger than the sharks normally encountered on feeds, they are an impressive sight and not afraid to bump divers. Grey Reef Sharks form part of their diet.

seen them at Sanganeb but the largest one that I ever saw was on Green Reef, southeast of Suakin. Visual estimation underwater isn't that accurate but it must have been around 4.5m (14.75ft) or so. The normally accepted maximum length for Tigers is 5.5m (18ft) with one record of 7.4m (24.28ft). Sanganeb has a

shoal of over 100 Scalloped Hammerheads and these are usually seen together off the North Point in the early morning. Then they break into smaller groups and follow the deep water along the East and South faces and arrive at the Southwest Point by early afternoon. There is a channel on the east side of the North Point that

Manta Rays

Manta Rays feed exclusively on plankton. They can be seen around all offshore reefs in the Red Sea throughout the year, but are common along coastlines in summer. As with Whale and Basking Sharks, they tend to feed in deeper water in the mornings and follow the plankton to the surface in the afternoon.

Manta Rays seem to be seen more in Sudan than Egypt but that may be due to the large number of divers in Egypt. They are not so common south of Sudan, however, because they are fished there. All offshore reefs in Sudan will have three or more resident mantas but Sanganeb and the Wingate Reefs complex both had at least nine while I was working the area, though this may have been due to the reefs' very large size. All have distinct markings that make individuals recognizable as permanent residents.

When feeding at the surface they prefer more sheltered waters and at Sanganeb and the Wingate Reefs complex, when there are very strong north winds in winter, all the resident Manta Rays congregate close to the reefs in the lee of their southern ends. This gives them both a relatively calm surface and plenty of plankton washed off the reef.

However, this gave me problems running a sport-diving operation as in really bad weather these were the only areas where I could give my clients a quality dive rather than in the lagoon. Approaching Sanganeb's Southwest Point on a windy December or January day was often fraught with difficulty, as Manta Rays seemed to be on the surface everywhere. I would have to gently manoeuvre the boat among them, taking care to safely moor the vessel in the strong wind without cutting any of the creatures with the boat's propellers. Once moored, the divers had to ensure that they did not land on a manta when they entered the water.

Once in, one would often have three mantas in sight but I never managed to achieve a good, clear picture due to the plankton.

One of the interesting things about mantas is that even the largest individuals jump about 1m (40in) completely out of the water. No one is quite sure why but one theory is that it is done to dislodge parasites.

I have often been on Sanganeb's southern deep-water jetty or on Towartit's Harvey Reef in the early morning and seen a large adult leap out of the water three or four times in succession, 30m (98ft) away. The loud slap as they fell back into the water attracted my attention. Size does not seem to matter either;

Above left The most common marine turtle seen in the Red Sea, Hawksbill Turtles are named after their hawk-like beak.

Above right Highly endangered, Green Turtles are less common in the Red Sea but common in the Arabian Gulf and the Gulf of Oman.

Opposite Manta Rays are usually loners but will congregate to breed or to feed in sheltered, plankton-rich water.

I have been loading up on the small boat jetty in Port Sudan harbour and seen a 50cm (20in) juvenile leap less than a metre away.

Many reefs have manta cleaning stations but not in surge channels as in the Maldives and Yap. When one is found, if divers act quietly the mantas will accept their presence and even 'bathe' in the divers' exhaust bubbles. Mantas attracted to plankton shown up by diver's lights at night often feed by performing slow head-over-heels, vertical loops. Sometimes they do this during the day when no plankton is obvious. I once had a client at 10m (33ft) on the first step of the North Point of Sanganeb, who had such

a wonderful time with a large manta performing vertical loops a couple of metres from him that he vowed never to dive again. He felt 'nothing could top that experience'.

Mantas are loners for much of their life but have to find a mate to breed. In August groups of 15 or so are found nose-to-tail in the shallow waters around Mesharifa and Gad Mesharifa Islets east of Sudan's Muhammad Qōl, and in nearby Dungunab Bay.

It is quite common to find mantas on the surface in the outer lagoon at Sanganeb in the afternoon, where they are happy to accept the attention of snorkellers. They can be found anywhere in Egyptian waters but particularly good sites in the summer months are Ras Nusrâni, Sha'b Sharm, Rocky Islet, the southern plateau of Big Brother Island and the southern plateau of Sha'b Maksur at Fury Shoal.

Marine turtles

Turtles are seen all year round on healthy reefs in the Red Sea but the species encountered most is the Hawksbill. The second smallest of the

marine turtles, Hawksbills ignore divers and just carry on with whatever they're doing; they are often encountered on wrecks where they feed on sponges. Green Turtles are much larger but are becoming increasingly rare. They require sandy sea grass areas but these are not the areas where most divers choose to dive.

All marine turtles require sandy beaches, preferably with shade, on which to nest so Green Turtles are more likely to be seen near sandy bays or islands. There are protected beaches for them in Saudi Arabia but for general divers a good spot to see them is Gezîret Zabargad (St John's Island, once known as Topazion, where topaz was once mined and which gives the gemstone its name), in southern Egypt. Loggerhead and Olive Ridley Turtles are rare in the Red Sea and Leatherback Turtles even rarer.

Five species of marine turtles are found off Oman, where Green, Hawksbill, Loggerhead and Olive Ridley Turtles nest. Leatherback Turtles do not nest there but are found off the Hallaniyat islands.

SEYCHELLES

A true mecca for viewing Whale Sharks

Fiona McIntosh

Some days the gods smile on us. I had one of those days diving on the picturesque jumble of boulders that make up the tiny island of L'Îlot, just off the northern tip of Mahé, the largest island in the Seychelles archipelago.

We had enjoyed an amazing dive admiring the profusion of colourful corals, while swimming through natural passages and happily photographing turtles nonchalantly grazing when, as we moved away from the rocks into more open water to ascend to the boat, the dive master signalled to us to keep still. A vast, dark shape was approaching like a submarine on a stealth mission. The outline became clearer until we could pick out its spots as the Whale Shark cruised past only metres below the surface. The sight of this magnificent fish was so unexpected that I could feel the adrenaline pumping as I tried to hover, and the effortless grace of the creature will be imprinted forever on my mind.

There are a few special spots in the world where divers can regularly encounter these gentle giants of the ocean. The ocean around Mahé is one, but while

Whale Sharks are known to congregate in the waters off the island – particularly between August and October when there are plankton blooms – chance encounters on scuba are not common. Occasionally a shark will approach and even play with the bubbles exhaled by divers but these interactions are normally quite short – naturally, the creatures are far more interested in finding food. As we returned to the dive centre we swapped stories. Other divers had seen Whale Sharks around the St Anne Marine Park nearby, and off Conception Island in the north. The dive master had heard several reports of good sightings off South Point and the Plantation Club in the south.

Although the Whale Shark is the world's largest fish, measuring up to 12m (39ft) and weighing up to 35 tonnes, very little is known

Opposite *The magnificent Whale Shark, the largest fish in the sea.*

Below *Remoras use a sucking disc on the top of their heads to hitch a free ride on Whale Sharks.*

about its behaviour and ecology. Migratory and slow growing, it feeds predominantly on zooplankton and small fish.

Few females are seen, most sightings being of juvenile males, and evidence indicates that the species is in decline as a result of human impact. This is particularly as a result of fishing to supply the lucrative shark-fin industry and 'Tofu Shark', as it is known in Taiwan because of its soft, white flesh. Their plight is exacerbated by the fact that there is no international protection for these magnificent creatures.

Many of the earliest recorded sightings of Whale Sharks were from the Seychelles. In the earliest days of colonization, the Marion Dufresne expedition (1768) and Captain Philip Beaver RN (1805) noted the presence of the species around the inner islands of the group and the regular sightings led to the launch of a formal research programme, the Whale Shark Monitoring Programme, in 1996.

The programme, largely run by the Marine Conservation Society, Seychelles (MCSS), assesses the occurrence and distribution of

Whale Sharks by aerial and boat-based surveys. Since the surface swimming habits of the sharks means that encounters on snorkel are easy, paying visitors are allowed to help the scientists with the research and the funds are channelled back into the programme. I had signed up to accompany the scientists that afternoon.

There was a buzz of excitement as we were briefed. The project's aims and background were explained and we learnt the key features of identification, the shark's feeding habits, its migration patterns, and what we could do to help the scientists in their research.

Tasks were allocated and as the principles of tagging were explained the MCSS scientist, David Rowat, tactfully suggested that we stay out of the line of fire between his tagging spear gun and the Whale Shark! The atmosphere was electric as we climbed onto the boat.

Fifteen minutes later the radio crackled into life. High above us in a microlight, the spotter guided us in.

'Whale Shark, seven metres long, five metres down, one o'clock, nine hundred metres.' As the

skipper turned the boat six snorkellers checked their masks and swung their legs over the side, ready to slide into the water on command. The boat slowed down.

'Three hundred, two hundred, one hundred, Whale Shark just left of the bow. Go.'

Rowat slipped into the water and we followed, trying to avoid making a splash. The skipper barked directions and we finned frantically to where Rowat had already dived, spear gun ready, to tag a new specimen. The huge fish was below us, effortlessly gliding along 10m (33ft) away.

We descended, trying to get level to take photographs. To be so close to this majestic

creature was incredible but the animal soon tired of our presence and, accompanied by its retinue of small pilot fish and remoras, it disappeared effortlessly into the depths.

Exhausted but exhilarated, we climbed back onto the boat and took our places at the bow as the other six divers on the day's encounter prepared for their first foray. We could hear the microlight overhead. Again the radio crackled and we raced to the scene.

This time the shark hung around for several minutes and we watched with envy as the second group climbed back on board, beaming from the thrill of the encounter and panting with exertion from the struggle of

keeping up with the shark. On our next dive we were even luckier and enjoyed a full 10 minutes of prime viewing during which we were able to relax and record the essential details – the size, shape of the fins, the accompanying fish – that the researchers seek to aid identification.

It was a privilege to all of us to feel part of such important research.

Opposite *The blunt nose and vast bulk of a Whale Shark is very distinctive – almost like a huge jet passing overhead*

Below *Whale Sharks are filter-feeders which consume vast amounts of zooplankton and small fish.*

CENTRAL MOZAMBIQUE

The mantas of the Mozambique Channel

Fiona McIntosh

If you want to see Manta Rays, Manta Reef, 12km (7 miles) north of Guinjata Bay, in central Mozambique, is a good place to start.

The reef sits right in the current, and current-borne nutrients pour over it, luring in mantas, which swoop by in their dozens.

Three cleaning stations on the reef virtually guarantee you'll see these incredible animals, which seem to follow a recognized flight path over the area as wrasse, butterflyfish and sergeant majors deftly pluck parasites from their mouths, gills and skin. Sometimes the rays hang, virtually motionless, at an angle in the current – as if in ecstasy at the sensation of being gently nibbled – allowing divers to see right through their gaping gills. The dive master becomes a traffic controller, directing awe-struck divers into canyons and gullies so as to avoid near collisions and the risk of scaring off the rays.

It is their sheer size that is so awesome – the largest have wingspans of over 6m (20ft) – and they are seriously intimidating as they 'fly' overhead or swim up to check you out.

On my first dive on Manta Reef two vast females floated by as we descended. Though thrilled by the experience, I feared that was it for the dive – and I hadn't even managed to set up my camera. Within minutes, however, we were on the first cleaning station, while the distinctive delta shapes cruised above, their mouths wide open as they filtered the plankton-rich water. The mouths of the approaching rays look huge thanks to two cephalic lobes. These extend, pincer fashion, in front of the manta's mouth and images of being swallowed whole flashed by.

By definition the presence of manta food means particle matter in the water but the visibility was around 12m (40ft), so we found a good vantage point and watched in wonder,

Opposite Cephalic lobes aid the manta in directing zooplankton into its mouth.
Below The distinctive black markings on the bellies of Manta Rays makes identification easy.

soon identifying individual rays by their bite scars, fin detail and the distinctive black markings on their underbellies. We had been told in the briefing that the best technique was to breathe slowly, keep still and wait; then the mantas will often approach. And sure enough they did, eclipsing the sun as they passed within a metre of our heads, so close that we often had to duck out of the way.

It was heart-stopping stuff and as we snapped away happily we were relieved that flash-photography did not scare them off.

Quite the contrary, in fact – they seemed intrigued by the noise of the strobes recycling and made yet more 'fly-pasts'.

I dived Manta Reef three more times, often hanging in the 'Canyon' or on the 'Pinnacles' just to watch the mantas, before I realized the beautiful reef offers many other delights. We spotted big Potato Groupers (known locally as Potato Bass), turtles, moray eels and huge shoals of colourful Snappers, Zaizer's Bigeyes (known locally as Crescent-tail Bigeyes), bait-fish and hunting kingfish on

every dive and many unusual nudibranchs including beautiful Spanish Dancers.

The variety of fish and coral life is incredible and this, coupled with the magnificent topography of pinnacles, ensures that even if you do not see mantas it is still an outstanding reef.

At 17–32m (55–105ft) Manta Reef is an advanced dive site and there are several other relatively deep dive sites in the area, such as Green Tree, where mantas are spotted just as regularly. Sightings even on the house reef are not uncommon. The icing on the cake is that Whale Sharks are also spotted regularly between December and March – often coming up to investigate the dive boat and allowing snorkellers to swim along-side them. Manta Rays and Whale Sharks on one dive is quite something – and the good news for non-divers is that most of the local resorts run snorkelling and Whale Shark viewing trips. While keeping up with a Whale Shark is quite an endeavour, snorkelling with such a colossus, the largest fish in the sea, is the trip of a lifetime.

KWAZULU-NATAL, SOUTH AFRICA

Sharks, as far as the eye can see

Fiona McIntosh

Sharks awaken our deepest, darkest fears, just as their sheer power and grace thrills us. It is these sensations that make shark interactions such a major dive attraction – and South Africa's East Coast, from the Eastern Cape to the Mozambican border, offers some of the best shark interactions in the world.

A top destination for shark *aficionados* is just south of Durban at Aliwal Shoal, where divers can expect sightings any time of the year.

Spotted Raggedtooth and Tiger Sharks are the most common species, while exciting encounters with Bull Sharks, known locally as Zambezi Sharks, draw divers to Protea Banks, slightly further down the coast near Scottburgh.

Anyone who has dived Aliwal Shoal will confirm it's high on adrenaline. The launch directly off the beach from the seaside town of Umkomaas is through crashing surf that tests even the strongest nerves, and the boat ride in a rigid inflatable boat (RIB) is often rough and wet. Our choice of Raggie Cave as our first dive site left no doubt as to what we were seeking, and as we descended, the incredible topography of the reef, with its undercut ledges, overhangs and swim-throughs, raised our spirits.

This is ideal 'raggie' country, and it wasn't long before we glimpsed our first – most beautifully framed in a large chamber.

We sank gently until just off the sand and hovered, noting the scars on its dorsal fin and the raw power of the awesome creature as it circled above us.

We spotted five more raggies on the dive, and yet more on a night dive later on, their beady eyes shining brightly in the torch-light. Spotted Raggedtooth, Sand Tiger and Grey Nurse Shark, are all common names for *Carcharias taurus*.

Docile by day, avoiding interaction where possible, their behaviour changes after dark – when they actively seek association with divers. It's scary stuff, diving 5km (3 miles) offshore with sharks hunting around you, but most of all it is a privilege.

We had been well-briefed in responsible diving and shark protocol – conservation of this precious resource is high on the agenda of the dive operators who are mindful of days when the sharks were more numerous. Even now, in the peak months you can see up to 30 raggies in Raggie Cave alone. If you don't see them there you can always drift down Shark Alley to Cathedral, one of the Aliwal Shoal's premier sites and another raggie hangout, with its dramatic arch rising from the seabed at 27m (89ft) to around 18m (60ft). Unfortunately the shoal's popularity has meant that there are some divers who do not respect the popular residents, crowding them out, shining torches in their eyes and making them wary of intruders.

Raggies typically arrive at the shoal in mid–late June as part of their migratory pattern, but some are permanent residents, particularly at Raggie Cave and Cathedral. Although this is the best-known species found on the shoal, they're not the *only* species you might see, so don't be surprised if you also see hammerheads, Great Whites and Bull (Zambezi) Sharks. The interest in diving with Tiger Sharks, which frequent the shoal from late January to June, has led to a new shark-diving industry with sophisticated baiting techniques. In many ways this is similar to Great White Shark cage-diving – without the cage!

Strong currents at Eelskin, at the southern-most tip of the shoal, make this a popular spot – one of the few places in the world where divers can dive freely with Tiger Sharks.

Usually the bait is placed on the seabed at 15–17m (45–52ft) and then the sharks are observed as they come to feed (usually in twos and threes) often passing within a metre (40in) of the watching divers.

Not surprisingly, various other sharks, fish and rays usually cruise in for a free lunch or to check out the action, so even if the tiger viewing is disappointing, the overall experience is always worth it. The alternative is sub-surface drifting, which usually results in even better sightings.

The boat is anchored and the water chummed with mashed sardines until a Tiger Shark approaches. After it has got used to the boat, and you have got your topside shots, a bait bucket is suspended under a marker buoy and released. Divers form a semicircle at a distance of 5m (16ft) around the bucket then drift along enjoying the show. It is easy diving but, in addition to enthusiasm and a healthy respect for sharks, you need good buoyancy as the long drift

Left An underwater photographer gets up close and personal with a Tiger Shark.
Opposite The distinctive, dramatic silhouettes of shoaling juvenile Scalloped Hammerhead Sharks passing overhead.

dive takes place between 4–6m (13–20ft). And be warned, Tiger Sharks are particularly fond of light colours (and silver striped fins) and will actually come up close and 'sniff' them. So if you're a nervous diver, dress down.

Adrenaline junkies should drive an hour southwest to the deep, dark and exciting diving of Protea Banks. Two pinnacles rise from the seabed, 8km (5 miles) offshore, creating an exposed reef with a raging current and plenty of big stuff to enthral even the most jaded individual. This is macho diving at its finest; the incredibly thorough dive briefing alone gets you into a state of high excitement. There's a very good reason for the briefing: divers have got lost on Protea so absolute adherence to dive plans and the carrying of surface marker buoys (SMBs) are a must. Dives are commonly made to between 10–30m (33–100ft).

Visibility can be down to a few metres, and then those dark shapes at the edge of your peripheral vision are pretty spooky and there's always the chance that a Bull (Zambezi) Shark will come in for a closer look.

If that hasn't scared you off, Protea can be one of the most rewarding dives of your life. Try to dive both the north and south pinnacles; both have incredible topography and surprisingly lush coral as well as a wide variety of colourful fish. Drift dives are the norm so you will not linger in any one spot – rather you should keep your eyes on the open water, (particularly on your ascent) as this is home to a dozen shark

Above Respecting the Raggedtooth Shark's space is the key to a successful dive.

Opposite top Bull Sharks, also called Zambezi Sharks in this region, have a reputation for aggressive behaviour towards divers.

Opposite below The extraordinary profile of a Scalloped Hammerhead Shark, surely one of the most distinctive shapes in the ocean.

species – everything from Grey Reef, Thresher and mako to the occasional Great White. While nothing is ever guaranteed, regular divers report sightings of up to seven shark species and, in season, 200 raggies on one dive!

The best time to go for hammerheads is November to May, for Spotted Raggedtooths June to October, for Bull (Zambezi) October to May and for Tiger Sharks, April and November, but chance encounters happen all the time in

the big blue. Further north, South Africa's premier diving location, Sodwana Bay, is a great place to see the gestating female raggies from December to March. The warm water, reasonable visibility – often in excess of 20m (66ft) – and short boat ride to Quarter Mile Reef make for superb, easy viewing and I would recommend this as a 'first ever' shark dive. You simply descend to the sand and wait, your heart pumping despite the lack of exertion, as up to 20 pregnant Spotted Raggedtooth Sharks cruise gracefully around and above you.

It is a beautiful, spiritual experience, though high on adrenaline; I have seen several divers head for the surface overcome with fear at such close encounters.

As with all interactions, however, you will get the most from your dive if you first become *au fait* with the behaviour of the sharks you are hoping to encounter. Choose the season

and the conditions carefully according to the species you most want to see. A shark speciality course is a good option but most reputable operators will give a full briefing about the type of sharks you are going to meet, their diagnostic features and behaviour.

Following the basic rules of diving with sharks and other large pelagics not only enhances your own experience but will ensure that others too can enjoy such interactions in the future.

Above all, observe. Do not disturb.

Keep out of caves, gullies, overhangs and the sandy patches on the reef where sharks are resting. Most importantly, do not block a shark's exit or force it towards the reef, do not touch, and do not approach them too closely.

Sharks are naturally inquisitive so just relax and hover, breathing slowly and gently and let them come to you. And when they do, have the camera ready – you'll get some great shots.

SOUTH AFRICA, SARDINE RUN
Pelagics at fever pitch – the Sardine Run

Doug Perrine

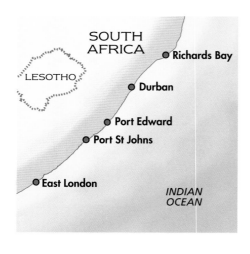

Along South Africa's East Coast, every year many residents are afflicted with a seasonal ailment they call 'sardine fever'. When shoals of snack-sized fish start washing up on the beaches of KwaZulu-Natal, locals take leave of their senses...

Normally sane, reserved people rush into the water to stuff fish into pockets, undergarments, or any convenient receptacle.

They skip school, desert work and forget their obligations. They get into fights over a catch worth a couple of cents. Generally they act like fools. They must catch the madness from the fish themselves, which leave a relatively safe and stable environment in the cool waters of the Cape region to migrate north into regions that are too warm for them to tolerate. Furthermore, to do so, they have to make use of cool counter-currents that fluctuate and are unreliable. Along the way hordes of furred, feathered, and scaly predators of every kind attack them without mercy. Millions are massacred. Yet every winter the fish mount another mass-suicide mission. Recently, the locals' malady has spread beyond South Africa, rapidly infecting large numbers of scuba divers, who now flock to South Africa in defiance of all conventional wisdom divers would be expected to use when planning a holiday excursion.

Let's take a closer look at the typical diving characteristics of South Africa's 'Wild Coast' during the Sardine Run season each June...

Poor visibility: check; rough seas: check; cold water: check; chance of poor weather: high; boating facilities: almost non-existent, requiring divers to push boats across beaches, sand bars, or other obstacles; danger level: high; comfort level: low; cost: high; chance of success: low; travel infrastructure: rather primitive in some

Opposite *Sharks zoom through rapidly opening tunnels in a bait ball of sardines, dealing death to laggards.*
Below *Common Dolphins force sardines to the surface and herd them into compact balls, upon which the dolphins and other predators can feed efficiently.*

areas. Let's face it, there is really not a great deal to commend it. So...

Why then are so many divers spending their hard-earned money for a good chance of a lot of frustration at considerable risk?

Simply put, it's for the small chance of experiencing a natural drama of unsurpassed intensity, guaranteed to awe and thrill even the most jaded observer of animal savagery.

Sardines are the ocean's coins – little oily bundles of concentrated food energy that offer the chance of life, growth, and reproduction to larger animals driven by greed or desperation. This is the gold rush that every predator in the ocean wants in on. Seabirds, dolphins and sharks migrate up the coast by the thousands. Their attacks churn large swathes of sea surface into white foam. Then there are the fur seals, baleen whales, tuna and other game fish that all follow the sardines up the coast. Even larger predators often stalk the sardine hunters...

Transient orcas have been known to charge into a shoal of sardines and seize dolphins and seals that let their guard down while attempting to snatch their sardine snack.

Diving in the middle of a furious feeding frenzy may seem like an insanely dangerous behaviour. It is.

There have already been serious injuries and life-threatening close calls on the Sardine Run, including shark bites and near-drownings. However, the white-knuckle surf launches may be the most perilous part of the experience. This is certainly not for the inexperienced, out-of-shape, faint-hearted, or impatient.

I include 'impatient' because most of the Sardine Run experience involves waiting around for something to happen, or the weather to break, or for a report from a spotter-plane.

Eyes in the sky are key to success in the whole experience. Small aircraft are the only way to efficiently survey the coastline and spot

the bait balls of sardines that have been forced to the surface, or pods of dolphins, migrating whales, or other activity of potential interest. It requires a skilled observer to recognize various forms of marine life from the air, ascertain their speed and direction of travel, and then direct boats to intercept them.

Most of the activity is extremely transient, so a boat generally has to be in the right place at the right time in order to arrive at an area of activity before it is over. Success demands expert interaction between a skilled boat captain, skilled pilot, and skilled divers.

The Sardine Run typically traverses a large stretch of South Africa's East Coast, from around East London all the way up to Durban or beyond. However, marine life and the sea conditions vary considerably along the coastline, as do facilities and infrastructure.

In the southern zone, between Port St Johns and East London, the action tends to be fast and furious, and fairly reliable from year to year. However, river runoff makes the ocean so dark and murky that it is very hard for divers to see anything.

Hence, the best viewing is often at the surface, watching the gannets dive and dolphins leap. From Port St Johns north to Port Edward, visibility is variable, and ranges from poor to fairly good. The action tends to move farther offshore in this region, and is less reliable. The sardines are mostly moving along the bottom, and only come to the surface when forced up by dolphins. When this happens, however, they tend to form classic bait balls, and divers are likely to see them under attack by dolphins, sharks, gannets, game fish, and sometimes seals and whales. Activity is spotty, however, and in rare years, sardines are hardly seen in this zone. If the conditions are not right, they may stay in the cool water down south, or they travel deep and offshore, bypassing the central zone as they make their way north.

Divers in the central zone play a waiting game, endlessly theorizing about what sort of weather conditions will get the sardines moving and to the surface.

Facilities in this region, the Wild Coast, tend to be more isolated and primitive. Nevertheless, underwater photographers and filmmakers favour it – because on those rare occasions when all the conditions come together perfectly, the visuals can be sublime.

From Port Edward to Durban, the water tends to be clearer and the diving conditions easier. Shoals may come right up on the beach

Left Copper or Blacktip Sharks dash through a bait ball, seizing mouthfuls of sardines.

Opposite top Gannets diving into a bait ball leave behind 'vapour trails' of small bubbles of air escaping from their plumage.

Opposite below When beach netters haul up their catch, local custom allows onlookers to snatch any sardines that fall from the net.

(where net fishermen are usually waiting), and sometimes stretch along the surface for kilometres. However, fewer predators travel this far north. Common Dolphins are not so prevalent in this region and since this is the species primarily responsible for causing bait balls, they are far less common here than elsewhere.

Divers' efforts are usually focused on finding bait balls, but they sometimes have second thoughts after they enter the water and find themselves being bumped and circled by Copper Sharks (also known as Bronze Whalers) while diving birds plunge into the water around them like a hailstorm of guided missiles.

Also exhilarating, but less terrifying, is to make an open ocean descent in the path of a pod of travelling dolphins. Hundreds may pass by in just a few minutes.

The drama and pageantry produced by this massive seasonal pulse of energy moving up the South African coast is equal to any other great natural spectacle.

THE MALDIVES
Seas of remarkable diversity

Rob Bryning

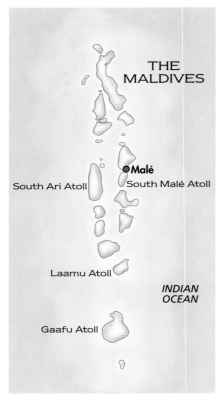

THE MALDIVES

South Ari Atoll

●Malé

South Malé Atoll

Laamu Atoll

INDIAN OCEAN

Gaafu Atoll

Two things will strike you on your first dive in the Maldives: the sheer numbers of fish, and their remarkable diversity. Reef life is prolific, with over 700 common fish species and many more still to be discovered and classified. When I first went to the islands in 1984, I was amazed at the sheer abundance of life the Maldives reef eco-system supports. But it was the Manta Ray that really captured my heart, for a meeting with one of these majestic creatures leaves you awe-inspired. A gentle and inquisitive creature, the manta moves through

the water with the grace of a large bird. Most certainly it doesn't deserve the incorrect, alternative name people call it in some countries – 'Devil Ray'.

My first encounter with a manta is very firmly etched in my memory. The dive site was Lankan Finolhu, only a short distance from the busy Hulhule Malé airport island, on the eastern atoll's outer reef and I stayed at the island of Kurumba. Then the resort itself was little more than just a few coral huts with thatched coconut-leaf roofs and a local boat cut in half, which served as the bar and reception. The island had a Swedish dive instructor who had a few tanks and an open-deck dive boat – a locally built *dhoni*, the traditional boat of the Maldives.

On this particular day the instructor very confidently announced that we were 'going to see the Manta Rays'. As a relatively novice tropical diver I was cynical and disinclined to believe that it was possible to really predict the

Opposite *Mantas Rays often seem to enjoy the sensation of divers' bubbles against their bellies.*
Below *Individuals are most easily identified by their ventral (belly) markings.*

movements of such a huge pelagic species. But an encounter with these elusive creatures was something I had craved so I followed the instructor with avid attention.

An hour later we arrived over the site on the outer reef of Lankan Finolhu Island, North Malé Atoll, where our instructor delivered a very clear dive briefing. We were told to stay together, not to go in front or deeper than the guide, stay low on the reef and at all costs, once we had ascended to the reef, avoid swimming in open water. The plan was to dive on the reef top at about 12m (40ft) and the dive master was totally confident that we would see Manta Rays, but he explained in no uncertain terms that if

we did not follow his instructions, we would frighten the mantas away and be disappointed.

We arrived at the cleaning station and, as if to order, a huge ray appeared out of the blue; a fantastic sight that awed us all. The manta began to circle the cleaning station and I thought this was too good to be true! Then, as I watched in wonder, I couldn't believe my eyes as a second, third and fourth manta came into the frame. I stayed, anchored to the spot, for an hour – and never had less than three enormous Manta Rays just a couple of metres away.

I couldn't help but ask what it was that drew the creatures in to this one particular site, for, during my one-week holiday, I dived at the site three times and each time we were treated to a spectacle. Each encounter was remarkable and a dream for every diver.

Now, 20 years later with considerable time spent observing these amazing animals, I know that this encounter was not luck.

Hundreds of dives with these magnificent creatures on this same dive site and many others like it have given me an insight into the behaviour and migration of Manta Rays. To find these animals in the first place you need a guide with a thorough and intuitive knowledge and understanding of the ocean currents and the monsoon winds of the Maldives as these are the two elements that determine the location of the mantas at all times of the year.

Being filter-feeders they eat plankton and other small organisms, but they need a great deal to survive as they span 4–6.7m (13–22ft) and can weigh over 1000kg (2200lb). Environmental conditions in the Maldives are perfect for rich plankton growth as the outer ocean reefs of the islands' atolls act as a barrier to the ocean currents, allowing layers of plankton to build up on the outer atoll wall and allowing an upwelling of plankton-rich water.

We know that there is a vertical migration of plankton over a 24-hour period. During daylight hours it is at a relatively deep level at around 100m (328ft) or so, but in late afternoon

and as night falls, the micro-organisms rise to the surface waters and disperse horizontally to feed. It is at night, when the plankton is at its most abundant at the surface, that the mantas spend most of their time feeding.

Then, having spent the night feeding, the mantas spend their daylight hours doing their house-keeping! Like many marine species, they are targeted by marine parasites that live on their gill filaments and abdomen.

They constantly try to get rid of these parasites to ensure their gills remain healthy but as they cannot reach the areas of skin most affected, they have to use cleaners to do the work for them. It is while the mantas are being cleaned that we, as divers, are able to enjoy our best manta encounters.

On the shallow tops of the ocean reefs, at a depth of usually no more than 10m (33ft), are massive coral heads. These attract a great variety of reef life, but more importantly they are also home to cleaner wrasse, which provide such an important service to the Manta Rays and other fish. These coral heads are the

equivalent of a car wash for the Manta Rays... Incredible to imagine, but true.

Drifting slowly on a gentle current these giants of the sea gracefully hover and circle the coral heads. Once relaxed and not under any threat, they open their huge mouths and the cleaner fish go to work. Dozens swim into the open mouth and start to pick off all the detritus, bugs and grubs that the previous night's feeding has collected. It is an amazing sight to be able to look right into a manta's mouth from just a metre or so away; you think you are going to be swallowed whole.

Competition for these cleaning stations is high, particularly in the early mornings. Mantas are very social animals congregating in large family groups of anything from 10–20 animals. After a busy night's gorging it is not uncommon to see 10, 14, 16 mantas, all circling and vying for the attention of the small colony of cleaner fish, each no bigger than your little finger.

After a while the mantas become aware of the diver's air bubbles and you might think this would frighten them off, but they seem to enjoy

the feeling of the bubbles on their bellies as they cruise by and will usually come back for more. Sometimes they become so accustomed to the diver, and fond of this tickling sensation, that they hover right over your head for several minutes. It is a remarkable encounter that leaves the diver with the feeling that a very special communication has taken place.

Sometimes the current pattern changes and the current sweeps into the atoll through the narrow channels of the outer reef wall, the food source is funnelled toward the surface and it is in these conditions that the mantas abandon their daily cleaning activities and start to feed again. They have a well-adapted method of feeding to ensure they can capture the enormous quantities of food they need to survive. On either side of the mouth are two cephalic fins, which sweep the plankton-rich water in the right direction.

These fins curl and uncurl according to the activity taking place, so if the mantas are feeding they will be stretched out to increase the surface area and thereby the potential to capture food. They are curled up like croissants when feeding is finished, lending a more streamlined effect. During feeding, the family group will swim in a circular pattern and it is best to snorkel rather than scuba dive with them as, at this point, the diver's bubbles disturb them. Possibly this is because the bubbles disperse their food source.

As our understanding of the behaviour of Manta Rays has developed, it has lead us to apply the same theories to understanding the behaviour of another giant, plankton feeding pelagic creature, the Whale Shark.

The Maldives has a large number of Whale Sharks in its waters and now that we are better able to predict their movements, we see them remarkably regularly. We are not sure if these animals are permanently resident or part of a migration but we see them throughout the year. Of course, it is the same

Above The filter-feeding Whale Shark is the largest living shark, they are common in the Maldives.
Opposite Manta Rays consume in the region of two per cent of their body weight every day, feeding on microscopic plankton.

plankton food source that attracts the Whale Sharks to the reefs but I also believe that they have the necessity to be cleaned just like the Manta Ray.

However, unlike the agile manta that selects a small cleaning station on huge coral blocks, the Whale Shark swims along the reef top passing over the various coral heads. This gives the resident cleaning fish a chance to swim up and grab a juicy morsel before the giant fish moves on.

In an area of reef that we call 'Whale Shark Alley' in Southern Ari Atoll, we have found a Whale Shark cleaning station just like the manta

cleaning stations. Curiously, many specimens we see are somewhat smaller than average, usually 7–8m (23–25ft), indicating that they are all juveniles. It is not uncommon to see three or more of them on the same section of reef and on one occasion I saw seven.

Our encounters with the largest fish in the sea tend to be as snorkellers rather than divers. If you are careful in your approach and you enter the water quietly and calmly (it's quite difficult to do when you are trying to contain your excitement at seeing a Whale Shark), you can watch these creatures for as long as you can snorkel. A 45-minute encounter is common, and the sharks will often appear to be very curious of your presence and will swim up to the surface to meet you.

I have filmed snorkellers backing away frantically as a 7m (23ft), 2000kg (4400lb) Whale Shark swims right up to them, large mouth agape. Then you can clearly see the look on

the snorkeller's face questioning if these Whale Sharks *really* do only eat plankton?

I have, on occasions, seen angelfish swim up to the shark and pluck a parasitic copepod from its leathery skin. For sure, cleaning is one of the elements that attracts these giants to the reef but there is another theory to be considered too. It is thought that as Whale Sharks spend a great deal of time in the chilly depths of the ocean it is possible that during the day they come onto the reefs to warm up.

There is still a great deal to be learnt about both Manta Rays and Whale Sharks and there is something about these pelagic animals that is quite awesome and I feel hugely privileged to have spent so much time in their company.

The more we learn about Manta Rays and Whale Sharks, the more easily we can predict their movements; by respecting their environment we can ensure they are protected and continue to appreciate and understand them.

THAILAND

Much more than reefs teeming with life

Paul Lees

Thai waters are renowned for their diversity of marine life and reefs that teem with a multitude of inhabitants in all shapes and sizes.

But there's actually a lot more than just pretty reefs to see and experience in the plankton-rich waters around the country.

A number of areas in both the Andaman Sea, off the country's western coast, and the Gulf of Thailand, lapping the opposing shores, seem to be on the regular routes of many pelagics including Whale Sharks and Manta Rays. Between these two oceans is a long list of now established diving destinations where these magnificent creatures can be seen, some on such a regular basis that encounters with these gentle giants have come to be somewhat expected.

Some destinations, particularly those in the Andaman Sea, are even fortunate enough to boast encounters with both of these graceful creatures. Naturally, given the abundance of marine life in these waters, any of these sites are also great places to encounter other species, including enormous shoals of trevallies and tuna, while others have hanging formations of smaller barracuda and small groups of Great Barracuda.

Andaman Sea – West Coast

Two of the top dives in the Andaman Sea are around the neighbouring open ocean sites of Hin Daeng (Red Rock) and Hin Mouang (Purple Rock). As these are the only two reef structures in the immediate area, they have become appointed feeding grounds for, among others, barracuda, rays, trevallies, sharks and kingfish. Over the years it has become quite

Opposite *The manta, always majestic, never unwelcome, confidently seen. Part of a wish list realised in Thai waters.*

Below *Capturing pelagics on camera can be enjoyed by all levels of divers, and is a great way of taking memories home with you after the dive.*

apparent that the big animals tend to favour either one of these two sites at any one given time, but not both. So if you are able to do so, it's suggested you should check out each one.

There is a possibility of strong and swirling currents, which can rapidly change intensity and direction, rendering them redundant as navigational aids. But this aside, this remains as one of the best diving destinations the country has on offer, and it's also among the deepest, with depths registering below 70m (230ft).

Hin Mouang is a completely submerged series of adjoining pinnacles forming an undersea plateau. The site is so named as it hosts a rich garden of purple sea anemones, which carpet the upper surface of the predominant pinnacle. A number of narrow valleys cut through the rock provide shelter for Coral Trout, Red Snappers and Oriental Sweetlips, while lionfish adopt the same waters as hunting grounds. Smaller crevices provide thoroughfares

for Banded Sea Kraits and Giant Moray Eels. The rocky structure is also home to a copious amount of scorpionfish and stonefish, all lying incognito, so divers need to keep their eyes open, and not just for the giants!

Hin Daeng differs in that it breaks the surface at low tide. The diversity of everyday reef life is also grand and ranges from tiny invertebrates and crustaceans such as Porcelain Crabs, Hinge Beak Shrimps and Golden Wentletrap Snails. There's also a variety of moray eels and sweeping shoals of snappers. In the depths it is worth inspecting the corals for Longnose Hawkfish and deeper still Grey Reef Sharks patrol along the seabed.

The best way to encounter pelagics at both of these sites is similar: move around. There is no telling where the visitors will pop up next.

Many divers have 'missed out' on Whale Shark and Manta encounters as they were only concentrating on a single expanse of water.

I am guilty of this myself; I was once keenly observing an enormous school of Red Snappers, only to find out that a Whale Shark passed right behind me!

These two world-class dives are accessed by day trips and live-aboard excursions from the dive centres on the islands of Koh Lanta, Phi Phi and Phuket, as well as those operating on the beaches in Krabi on the mainland.

Heading north, the two limestone karsts of Koh Bida Nai and Koh Bida Nok sit in the Andaman Sea immediately south of Koh Phi Phi Ley. These are both popular sites for spotting all of these impressive creatures, and they are also served by all the operators.

To the northwest of Koh Phuket lie the Marine National Parks of Mu Koh Similan and Mu Koh Surin. Both are on the favoured lists of day trips and live-aboard excursions. Mantas seem to prefer the waters around the Similans and the islands of Koh Bon and Tachai to the north, whereas Whale Sharks tend to cruise the waters around Surin, particularly

Richelieu Rock. This 'pelagic magnet' attracts enormous shoals of trevallies and barracuda.

The best diving around Koh Bon concentrates around the southwestern side of the island.

It's always worth peering away from the hues of soft corals to see what's behind you in the blue water. Manta Rays are drawn into these surroundings more often than not, and in no particular regularity of depth! The reef here features a series of small 'wall-like' sections, which make terrific places to simply rest and wait for the mantas as they soar in and out of the surroundings.

To the north, Koh Tachai is a series of underwater plateaus in a variety of depths off the southern end of the verdant island. The

outermost and deepest of the ledges features large boulders and rocks; providing great swim-throughs and has been adopted as a home by a number of different species of sharks, including Leopard and nurse.

However, it's not just the marine life residing around the reef that attracts divers to this site, the waters above and beyond these rocky structures are also noteworthy. If the visibility range is not at its best there's a good chance that enormous filter-feeders such as Manta Rays and Whale Sharks are in the area somewhere, and not always singularly.

Richelieu Rock is primarily composed of a very substantial rocky structure, complemented by rocky 'turret-like pinnacles' around the

perimeter of its upper surface; the tallest of which breaks the surface at low tide. There are many shelves and ledges at all depths, making this (conditions permitting) an extremely enjoyable and interesting site suitable for all levels of diver.

The rock has become legendary for its number of visiting Whale Sharks, and as it is the

Opposite *The good news is that encounters with Whale Sharks can be enjoyed off both coastlines, and at a number of exciting diving destinations.*
Below *Divers can literally engulf themselves in healthy shoals of Giant Trevallies at a number of diving destinations in the Andaman Sea and the Gulf of Thailand.*

only food source in the area it is an excellent place for spotting a wide range of predatory pelagics including Rainbow Runners, Chevron and Great Barracuda, Giant, Golden and Threadfin Trevallies and Dogtooth Tuna. And it's not just the surrounding waters that are worth watching as closer inspection of the rocks' inhabitants reveals all manner of interesting interactions. For example, there are gardens of sea anemones with a variety of hosts, such as crabs and shrimps.

As a footnote, the island of Koh Bon, just to the north of the Similans, has the highest number of Manta Ray encounters in the country. Richelieu Rock, in its turn, lays claim to the greatest frequency of Whale Sharks, which on many occasions are in pairs.

Gulf of Thailand – East Coast

At the top of the list of diving areas in the Gulf of Thailand is the island of Koh Tao and as far as pelagic encounters are concerned, the site of Chumphon Pinnacles, 14km (9 miles) to the northwest of Nang Yuan Island is hard to beat. The site consists of four underwater pinnacles which tower up from around 34m (112ft). The highest one stops 16m (52ft) before the surface.

This is an ideal site for pelagic spotting, healthy shoals of Bigeye and Giant Trevallies, mackerel and tuna. Whale Sharks are often sighted here during the preferred diving season's early and later months, with their travelling partners, the pilot fish and remoras.

Between Koh Tao and to the south the island of Koh Phangan sits Sail Rock. Dive operators from these two islands and the international tourist destination of Koh Samui, further south, regularly serve this, probably the finest dive site in the Gulf of Thailand. The dive itself follows a route around a small rocky outcrop, which radiates outwards once beneath the surface. Although Sail Rock is generally not considered to be suitable for inexperienced

divers to independently explore, the local dive operators all provide qualified dive leaders.

The rock's central formation plummets to the seabed in the form of a submerged tower block, although it does feature a series of walls interspersed by ledges, all heavily punctuated with bushy black corals, sea whips and stinging hydroids. There is also a natural 'chimney', which provides you with a most enjoyable, vertically inclined swim-through. This, and the handful of surrounding pinnacles are all very rich in the amount and diversity of reef inhabitants.

Furthermore, they all afford splendid underwater vistas of the passing marine life, which includes an impressive representation of pelagic visitors, especially during the months of August

and September when there are, along with the occasional Manta Ray, frequent Whale Shark sightings. This is a site not to be missed.

The islands and islets off Chumphon Town on the mainland are also frequented by the world's biggest fish. The northernmost chain of outcroppings in the area, Hin Lak Ngam is possibly one of the most overlooked Whale Shark dives in the country.

During the preferred diving season it can be favourably compared to a number of destinations off the opposite coastline. Down south, closer to the border with Cambodia is the island of Koh Chang, Thailand's second largest island.

Whale Sharks are known to visit the local waters, particularly at Koh Rang Pinnacles.

WESTERN AUSTRALIA

Where Whale Sharks are just a fin-kick away

Rochelle Mutton

The subtropical sea that laps against Western Australia is the most reliable place in the world to swim alongside the king of sharks. With a massive dorsal fin and cavernous mouth, the Whale Shark is the ultimate big fish that anyone can experience by simply stepping off a charter boat.

In a rush of bubbles, the topside blanket of blue is transformed into a widescreen view of a shark about the size of a bus – and it's heading your way. Its colossal dark form, covered in white spots, sparkling in the sun, is one of the most spectacular and beautiful sights to grace the world's oceans. It's amazing that these migratory giants, one of the ocean's largest life forms, feed on the sea's smallest, plankton and small fish that they filter from the sea, as they cruise through tropical and warm-temperate regions.

Between April and June each year Whale Sharks gather along the 260km (162 mile) Ningaloo Reef that hugs Australia's North West Cape. No other place in the world has such predictable sightings of these magnificent creatures, and this has spawned a multi-million dollar ecotourism industry on one of the world's largest fringing reefs.

Further along the coast to the north and south are a number of island clusters. These include the Abrolhos, Montebello and Dampier Archipelago groups, and each has its unique balance of sharks, game fish, and, in the case of the latter two groups, breeding turtles as well. Located in remote northwest Australian waters, beyond Australia's continental shelf, the Rowley Shoals are a Holy Grail for divers, with an

Opposite *It may be the king of sharks but as a filter-feeder, the Whale Shark is one of the safest ocean giants to swim alongside.*

Right *A school of Giant Trevallies shows off their streamlined shape to perfection.*

Below *A Manta Ray flies gracefully through shoals of fish on the reef.*

amazing concentration of marine life supporting many pelagic species. Collectively, these largely unspoiled marine regions make Western Australia a prime destination for experiencing the company of sea creatures at the top of the ocean's food chain.

While Whale Shark dives quite naturally take top billing and require only the ability to snorkel, Ningaloo Reef's swirling kaleidoscope of tropical life attracts a rich bounty of big fish that divers will enjoy.

The winter peak season is 25–35°C (77–95°F) and the arid climate has little fresh water runoff. This helps to preserve the coral ecosystem that attracts hungry Whale Sharks and Manta Rays.

The skippers of Whale Shark charters head out to the reef early each morning, staying in radio contact with light aircraft that act as spotter-planes with the pilots looking for the tell-tale shapes of the giant filter-feeders at the

surface. While waiting for news from the skies, the charters run dives to 18–30m (60–100ft) for those with the relevant scuba certification. The deep melodic songs of Humpback Whales remind divers they are in the kingdom of giants. The gentle rhythm of shoaling fish explodes into a frenzied dash to safety in the coral, seconds before dozens of marauding Giant Trevallies charge the site for prey.

Gliding over the coral are the placid, acrobatic Manta Rays, with wingspans averaging 3m (10ft). Certain diving sites, most notably in Coral Bay, have 'cleaning stations', where mantas appear regularly to have cleaner

fish pick off parasites and loose skin. A sudden shadow over the station signals the arrival of a manta, eclipsing the sun. This is the best chance divers have of an intimate experience with a ray and if a diver stays still it's likely that a majestic ray will pass within touching distance several times.

Some dive charters are dedicated exclusively to snorkelling with mantas. These gentle but flighty creatures exhibit varying degrees of tolerance to human company. While instructions are given to swim behind or to the side of the creatures, and to avoid splashing, which could spook them, it generally takes a strong fin-kick and relaxed ray

for a snorkeller to be able to stay with it for more than 30 seconds. However the charter boats obligingly pick up snorkellers as soon as they lose sight of the cruising filter-feeder, and catch up with it for further encounters.

Manta Rays are most commonly found in the shallows of Coral Bay, or along the reef walls off Exmouth, where there is a gentle

Opposite *Remote tropical beaches on the Montebello Islands are a haven for nesting Hawksbill Turtles.*
Below *Swift schools of Yellowtail Kingfish dash over the reef hunting for fish.*

breaking swell. Snorkelling along such walls is also a great way to experience reef and Spotted Raggedtooth Sharks, (known locally as Grey Nurse Sharks). Every now and then, some manta tourists get more than they bargained for with the occasional Tiger or hammerhead shark also passing along the wall.

The more daring divers chasing the ultimate deep-water thrill will find charter operators willing to take them out to the open ocean to swim with full-sized pelagic sharks.

Such controversial and sporadic encounters use fish remains as bait to attract the sharks. Snorkellers hold onto a floating or buoyed line from the back (downstream) of the boat, to watch the fearsome yet curious hunters pass by. While the open-water experience sounds extreme, it is in this same environment that hundreds of tourists swim with Whale Sharks each week.

In the last 20 years, understanding of this environment and of Whale Sharks, has grown exponentially. Dr Geoff Taylor, the first scientist to study the Ningaloo Whale Sharks in the early 1980s, recalls how charter operators refused to take him beyond the reef shallows to swim with the Whale Sharks, as they feared he might be attacked by other shark species.

Much has changed since then, however: open-water swimming with this biggest of sharks has spawned an industry worth AU$12m annually. Certainly there is some comfort in knowing that in all the thousands of interactions with many shark species each year at Ningaloo, there has never been a fatality.

The local authorities, with input from charter operators, have drawn up strict guidelines to ensure tours have minimal impact on this threatened species. Snorkellers are split into two groups of eight, taking turns to be dropped off near to the shark's line of travel. First a leader, called a 'spotter', swims in line with the shark's pectoral fin, arm straight in the air as a marker on the creature's location. Then, when the dive co-ordinator shouts 'Go! Go! Go!' it is time for one group of divers to enter the water.

The gripping exhilaration of coming face to face with a Whale Shark has to be quickly followed by brisk fin-kicks to stay by its side. To avoid irritating the shark and causing it to dive, snorkellers are instructed to minimize splashing. They must also avoid swimming either in front of the pectorals or above the animal and should stay on the surface, at least 3m (10ft) away at all times, even if the creature chooses to be closer. Personal safety is also important, and while a Whale Shark may mean no harm, its considerable bulk and giant tail is capable of inflicting a serious injury.

Most divers are usually able to stay alongside the creature for about two to eight minutes, before regrouping to be picked up by the boat, alternating with the second group for turns at snorkelling with the shark.

Even though many studies have been carried out on Ningaloo's Whale Sharks in recent years, scientists still know little about the life of these ocean nomads, such as where they give birth or the exact influences on their migratory patterns.

They are thought to live for more than 100 years but, remarkably, may not become sexually active until they reach an age of about 50, when they are about 9m (29ft). Their vulnerability to a population crash is intensified by their migratory habits, taking them into dangerous waters... satellite tags suggest that Ningaloo's star attractions travel north to Southeast Asian waters where they are hunted by commercial fisheries and subsistence villagers. This can have a significant impact on their sustainability; a female Whale Shark slaughtered in a Taiwanese fishery was found be carrying 300 pups, averaging 54cm (21in).

Adult Whale Sharks are rarely seen anywhere in the world longer than 12m (39ft). The Ningaloo populations are 4–12m (13–39ft) and are mostly sexually immature males with unused claspers. Fortunately,

Right *A head-to-head encounter with a Blue Marlin is a thrilling experience never to be forgotten.*
Below *The flattened head of Scalloped and Great Hammerhead Sharks is referred to as a 'cephalofoil'.*

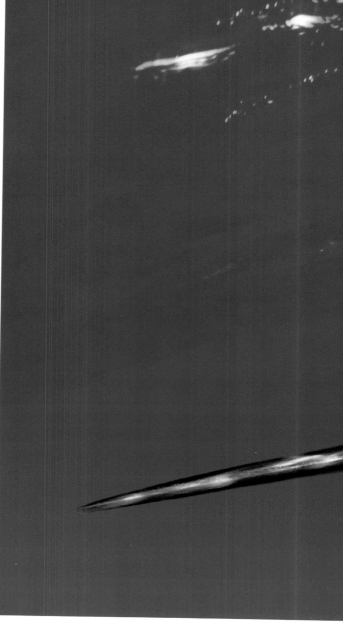

adult Whale Sharks have skin 15cm (6in) thick and few natural predators. They seem able to survive serious attacks. Photographs of a 5m (16ft) Ningaloo Whale Shark made headlines in the 2003 season after it lost of most of its dorsal fin in a single bite. The culprit was thought to have been a Great White straying from its usual southern environment.

Plenty of shark and other pelagic action can also be found around the hundreds of islands off the Western Australian coast. Halfway between Perth and Ningaloo lies a 100km (62 mile) matrix of underwater channels and canyons surrounding the 122 islands of the Abrolhos. These are fertile grounds for seeing species such

as Tiger Sharks, Australian Sea Lions, mackerel, Yellowtail Kingfish, dolphins and tuna. To the far north, islands such as the Montebellos, Barrow Island, the Lowendal island group and Dampier Archipelago, have similar species and sandy beaches, ideal for nesting turtles.

Away from mainland hazards such as predatory foxes and four-wheel-drive vehicles, four species of endangered turtles – Green, Hawksbill, Flatback and Loggerhead Turtles – nest in relative peace between October and April. Divers will regularly come across turtles all around the islands. Often the animals will be engaged in mating rituals, with dual heads breaking the surface. Isolation nurtures

marine populations and the Rowley Shoals, 330km (180 nautical miles) from Broome, thrive in an area protected from human exploitation and richly nourished by tropical currents. Rising from the seabed 230–444m (755–1457ft) below, the three coral shoals – Mermaid, Clerke and Imperieuse – support at least 233 coral species and 688 types of fish. In this deep-water environment, big sharks are reasonably common, with West End Wall, on the Mermaid shoal, being renowned for its hammerhead sharks.

The vibrant coral walls, which fall into a seemingly bottomless black, are also the domain of transient pelagics; mackerel, barracuda and tuna, are abundant and have a mild

inquisitiveness towards divers, distinct from the more timid mainland populations.

Perhaps the most unique place to experience billfish is in the fast tidal flows that rip through the narrow channels traversing the shoals. The swift water cushion carries free divers at breakneck speed, manoeuvring the body cleanly over reef boulders and around hairpin bends, to be picked up by the charter boat at the other end. On this exhilarating ride, divers chance upon spectacular game species such as marlin and sailfish.

In this rare experience divers can taste, just for a moment, what it is like as a sleek pelagic, in an effortless race across the underwater terrain.

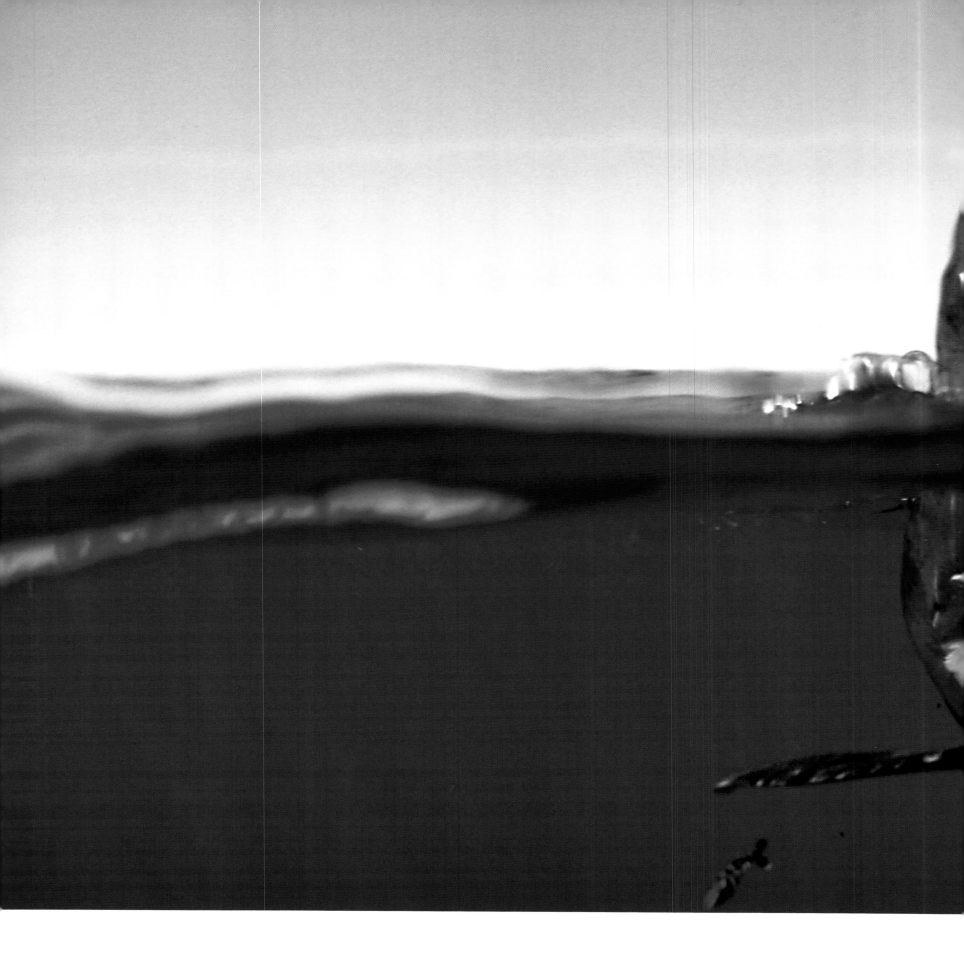

Above Oceanic Whitetips are among the most impressive of sharks to be seen in the Indo-Pacific but other species to be seen in the region include Scalloped and Great Hammerhead, Blue, Blacktip, Spinner, Bull, Tiger, Bluntnose Sixgill, Dusky, Thresher, and Shortfin Mako Sharks.

Indo-Pacific

MALAYSIA

Where pelagics abound

Jack Jackson

As with its neighbours, Indonesia and the Philippines, Malaysia is part of the Coral Triangle, which is at the centre of marine diversity in the Pacific.

Malaysia is best known for its smaller, reef species but it also has almost all of the pelagic species known to inhabit or pass through warm waters. So, whether you happen to be diving off Peninsular Malaysia or Borneo, the only difference is whether you are near deep water such as at Pulau Aur, off Peninsular Malaysia or Pulau Sipadan,

Terumbu Layang-Layang and other Malaysian islands and shoals in the Spratlys.

Whales, dolphins and pelagic sharks abound, and Manta Rays are common on offshore reefs. But where Malaysia stands out is the number of marine turtles encountered. More on them later...

Whales and dolphins

At least 21 species of whales and dolphins reside in or pass through the waters of Malaysian territorial and Exclusive Economic Zone (EEZ). The whales include Bryde's, Fin, Sperm, Pygmy Sperm, Cuvier's Beaked, Melon-headed, Pygmy Killer, False Killer, Killer, and Shortfin Pilots.

The dolphins to be seen include Rough-toothed, Indo-Pacific Humpbacked, Common Bottlenose, Indo-Pacific Bottlenose, Pan-tropical Spotted, Spinner, Common, Fraser's and Risso's. Irrawaddy as well as Finless Porpoises are also to be seen in these waters.

Cetacean species

A further eight species of cetaceans may occasionally be found: Humpback, Minke, Sei, Blue, Dwarf Sperm, Ginko-toothed, Beaked, and Blainville's Beaked Whales and Striped Dolphins. A two-week aerial survey off Sarawak recorded five sightings of filter-feeding Baleen whales, between Mukah and Tanjung Datu.

According to studies of strandings and through discussions with fishermen, it was found that the most common species are Irrawaddy and Indo-Pacific Humpback Dolphins, and Finless Porpoises, followed by Bottlenose and Spotted Dolphins.

In discussions with fishermen they claim accidental by-catches of dolphins and porpoises in their gill nets have declined. This decline in dolphin numbers may be due to the depletion of the fish resources, brought about by trawling, while there is also the decline in the quality of water flowing out from the main rivers due to coastal development and logging.

Dolphins can be seen in all Malaysian waters but they are more likely to be encountered when travelling to or between reefs.

Whale Sharks

Whale Sharks are the ocean's largest fish – one measuring 13m (41ft) was caught on November 11, 1949 off Baba Island, near Karachi, Pakistan. They can be found in large shoals or individually, often coming close inshore and even entering lagoons. They prefer areas where the surface temperature is 21–25°C (70–93°F)

with plankton-rich colder water upwelling such as at seamounts. Unlike Basking Sharks, Whale Sharks actively suck in their prey.

It is common to be photographing a macro subject at 20m (66ft) or more, when suddenly 'the sun goes out'. On looking up you see either a Whale Shark or a Manta Ray, but due to decompression problems you cannot ascend quickly to get close to the animal.

In Peninsular Malaysia this happened to me at Tiger Rocks on Pulau Tioman and when I got back to the resort a group of novice divers filled me in on their exciting encounter with the Whale Shark on the surface. The next day

this animal was joined by a Manta Ray at Magicienne Rock. Nearby, the north side of Pulau Chebeh and the northern end of Pulau Sepoi are also good for Whale Shark sightings.

However, Whale Sharks in Malaysian waters do not always stick to the script when it comes to seasons. The encounter described above happened in September – though the normal

Opposite *Divers often find a Green Turtle resting on stony corals under overhangs during the day.*
Below *Like most dolphins, Pan-tropical Dolphins like to surf.*

Above *Divers often interact with Blue Sharks near to the surface.*
Right *One should be wary when getting this close to a large Tiger Shark.*
Opposite *Snorkellers get close to a Whale Shark.*

season for this species at Pulau Tioman from is the months of March to May.

Elsewhere in Peninsular Malaysian waters Whale Shark encounters are common around the Johor Marine Parks, especially in deep water such as off Pulau Aur. Here, Rayner's Rock, northeast of Pulau Dayang, is a seamount 33m (100ft) high. Pinnacles on the east side of Pulau Aur, rising from 30m (98ft) to within 10m (33ft) of the surface. Pulau Redang is also a good locality, especially off Big Seamount.

In Malaysian Borneo, being close to Kota Kinabalu, it has long been known that Whale Sharks were found to be around Tunku Abdul Rahman Marine Park from November to April, when a build-up of plankton attracts krill, which in turn attracts the sharks.

However, the krill are so plentiful the water is brown and the visibility is awful.

In these conditions, close encounters with these colossal animals can be frightening as they suddenly loom out of the gloom. As many as 12 whale sharks have been spotted in the waters around Miri during the peak plankton season and now that there are many permanent resorts we find that there are often Whale Sharks at Pulau Sipadan and all waters north to Pulau Lankayan. April is the main season but they can appear at any time.

Whale Sharks migrate along the coasts of Sarawak and west Sabah during February and March every year, so the opportunity was taken to tag and track them by satellite. Unfortunately the tags were not reliable and only one animal was actually tracked continuously – for just two

months. Nevertheless, the information that was obtained was quite revealing.

The shark went from Kota Kinabalu to Labuan, Miri and Kuala Baram, then back to Labuan and then to Terumbu Layang-Layang… where the transmitter's battery failed and contact was lost.

Sharks

The chances of spotting the larger predatory sharks in Southeast Asia are not as good as in the Red Sea unless divers are in more remote areas near deep water. The sharks are still to be found around the shallower reefs but not in large numbers due to the effects of overfishing.

Again, your best chances of encounters are off Pulau Aur in Peninsular Malaysia or off Pulau Sipadan, Terumbu Layang-Layang and the other Malaysian islands and shoals in the Spratlys, off the coast of Borneo.

Two decades ago shark fisheries were restricted by the low average wealth of people in shark-consuming cultures and sharks

that were caught as by-catch were often released. Today, however, the average wealth of these people has increased, fishing methods have become more efficient, and shark fins have become very valuable.

They are dried and made into shark-fin soup, a traditional delicacy and a symbol of status in Southeast Asia. Malaysian traders import fins from over 25 countries and export to around 15 countries worldwide. The country is still one of the world's largest importers of shark fins with the most popular being those of Blue Sharks, followed by those of Blacktip, Sandbar and Hammerhead Sharks.

Pelagic sharks found in Malaysian waters include Scalloped and Great Hammerhead, Blue, Blacktip, Spinner, Bull, Oceanic Whitetip, Tiger, Bluntnose Sixgill, Dusky, Thresher, and Shortfin Mako Sharks.

Of these, the sharks most seen by divers are Scalloped Hammerheads, in small numbers off many of the other sites, and large shoals off Terumbu Layang-Layang and other

Above *Scalloped Hammerhead Sharks are spooked by the noise of exhaust bubbles and are more easily approached when using a rebreather.*
Opposite *Manta Rays are curious if you approach them quietly.*

shoals and islands in the Spratlys. Normally found below the thermocline, Scalloped Hammerheads will be closer to the surface when the water is cold or when chasing prey into the shallows. Divers are often spooked when these magnificent creatures chase their prey right up to the reef at Terumbu Layang-Layang, where the best time to see them is in the colder months of April and May.

More good sites for large shoals are the Royal Charlotte and Louisa Reefs to the south-west of Terumbu Layang-Layang. Large shoals are usually all females with the matriarch at the centre, whereas male Scalloped Hammerheads form small groups. Small groups are also found at Dallas Reef, north-northwest of Terumbu

Layang-Layang and Ardasier Reef, to the north-northeast of Terumbu Layang-Layang.

Oceanic Whitetip, Blue, Thresher, and Shortfin Mako Sharks are mostly found in open water off reefs in deep water. Threshers are common off the North and South Luconia Shoals south-southwest of Terumbu Layang-Layang and at Terumbu Layang-Layang itself. However, they do not get close enough to

divers for a good photograph. Bull Sharks are more likely to be seen near river outlets while Tiger Sharks can be seen anywhere, especially near ports.

Blacktip Sharks, which are not to be confused with the very common but smaller Blacktip Reef Sharks, are quite prevalent off reefs that are not quite so deep like those around Pulau Redang and Pulau Tioman.

Manta Rays

Manta Rays can be found anywhere in Malaysian waters as they are as at home in shallow water as over deep water.

As with Whale Sharks, their best areas for feeding on plankton are those where currents hit seamounts and the resulting colder water upwellings bring plankton into shallow water or where plankton is washed off reefs. Some of the reefs and shoals of the Spratlys have conditions similar to those found in the Maldives but elsewhere in Malaysian waters there is nowhere Manta Ray encounters can be guaranteed on any particular day.

In the Spratlys, Moody Reef, south-southwest of Terumbu Layang-Layang, North and South Luconia Shoals, Dallas and Ardasier Reefs, and Terumbu Layang-Layang, itself, are good sites for finding mantas. However, I have seen them everywhere from the Perhentian Islands to Pulau Aur off Peninsular Malaysia and from Sarawak around the northern end of Borneo to Pulau Sipadan in Borneo. Pulau Redang is good around the seamounts while one of the best areas for sightings is off Pulau Tioman. Surrounded by enormous volcanic rocks and boulders, the north side of Pulau Chebeh, Magicienne Rock, Tiger Rocks and the northern end of Pulau Sepoi, are all good sites.

At Pulau Aur, Rayner's Rock, northeast of Pulau Dayang, there is a 33m seamount where encounters with large Manta Rays are common. On the east side of Pulau Aur similar encounters occur at pinnacles that rise from 30m (98ft) to within 10m (33ft) of the surface.

Marine turtles

As mentioned in the beginning, Malaysia is justly famous for marine turtles so it's not surprising that Pulau Sipadan is often called 'the turtle capital of the world'. But there are many islands, both to its south off Indonesian Kalimantan, and to its north, where just as

many turtles nest. However, these islands are not dived as often, so the turtles are shyer.

Among these islands a group that straddles the border with the Philippines north of Sandakan, is collectively known as 'The Turtle Islands Park'. Here the turtles are protected on both sides of the border. In Malaysian waters, this park comprises Pulau Selingan, Pulau Gulisan and Pulau Bakkungan Kecil.

Six of the world's seven marine turtle species can be found in Malaysian waters: Green, Hawksbill, Loggerhead, Leatherback, Pacific Olive Ridley, and occasionally Flatback Turtles. Four of these – Green, Hawksbill, Leatherback and Pacific Olive Ridley Turtles – nest on Malaysian beaches. At Pulau Sipadan, they nest all year with the peak period being August when you can encounter 20–30 on a single dive. They are so used to divers here that they completely ignore them and simply carry on eating, sleeping or mating.

Protected turtle parks also exist off Sarawak on the west side of Borneo where five species of marine turtles are found: Green, Hawksbill, Olive Ridleys, Loggerhead, and Leatherback

Turtles. Major nesting areas are on the Sarawak Turtle Islands of Pulau Talang-Talang Besar, Pulau Talang-Talang Kecil and Pulau Satang Besar and Pulau Satang Kecil at Talang-Salang National Park. Other nesting localities include Tanjung Datu, Telok Melano, Samunsam Wildlife Sanctuary, Similanjau National Park, Kampung Puguh and Tanjung Batu in Sematan, as well as off Miri. The peak nesting time is May to October.

Satellite tagging of turtles that nested in Sarawak shows that after staying around the area for a while the creatures quickly migrate northeast, nearing Kota Kinabalu in nine days. They then travel around the northern tip of Borneo past Kudat to either Malaysian or Philippine waters northeast off the Sabah Turtle Islands Park. Here they take separate ways. Some continue south to Pulau Sipadan and then further south while others continue in Philippines waters to areas off the Tawi-Tawi Islands or north of Jolo Island.

Several of the islands such as Pulau Redang, Pulau Sipadan and Pulau Lankayan that have diving resorts also have turtle hatcheries.

Above A Green Turtle passing a shoal of Bigeye Trevallies.

Above left The English common name for the Olive Ridley marine turtle comes from the olive-green colour of its shell.

However, the government of Malaysia has now decreed that visiting divers cannot stay in accommodation on Pulau Sipadan but should stay on the nearby islands such as Pulau Mabul or Pulau Kapalai, or on a live-aboard boat and commute daily (15 minutes) to Pulau Sipadan.

The turtles most commonly encountered in Malaysia are Green and Hawksbills. Green Turtles are usually much larger than Hawksbills and are mainly nocturnal and herbivorous. When nesting they prefer remote islands with overhanging branches at the top of the beach,

where they can lay their eggs in the shaded, cooler sand under the vegetation.

For all but the Hawksbill Turtles, nesting is a slow and laborious process. Choosing a high tide and mostly at night, the turtle hauls itself up the beach.

In contrast, however, nesting Hawksbills are more agile and leave the water remarkably fast, some are able to rise on their flippers and move like a crocodile; they are mainly carnivorous and like to consume sponges.

On land, turtles appear to be shedding tears but they also do this at sea. These 'turtle tears' are believed to prevent the eyes from becoming dehydrated and cleanse them of sand. They also help the animal to excrete salt.

Leatherbacks differ from other species of marine turtles: they are much larger and their carapace is composed only of dermal ossicles.

The carapace is not fused to the underlying skeleton. Instead the ribs and backbone are embedded within it. This carapace looks like rather like brown leather and bears seven longitudinal ridges.

The Leatherback has a more streamlined shape and this, and its long flippers, enable it to swim at up to 10km/h (6mph) and cover large distances; migrations of 5900km (3650 miles) have been recorded.

In the 1960s a 20km (12 mile) stretch of beaches centred on Rantau Abang and nearby Kuala Abang, in Terengganu, was a major nesting area for Leatherbacks from May to September each year.

These beaches have a deep water approach, heavy surf and a steep slope. This means that the turtles have shorter distances to crawl up the beach to reach a nesting area that is sufficiently

far enough above the high-water mark and still free of vegetation. The nesting turtles became a tourist spectacle with an associated festival taking place in the months of July and August.

Now, however, the number of Leatherbacks here and on Pulau Tengah has dropped to a handful. It is tempting to think that the intrusion of tourists is the cause, but in fact only a small percentage of the nesting beaches were open to tourists, while the others were protected and had controlled turtle hatcheries. WWF Malaysia believes that the increased use of fishing nets is mainly to blame.

The numbers of nesting Leatherbacks have declined all around the world but, you can still see them in Malaysian waters, especially along the east coast of Peninsular Malaysia. I have myself been fortunate to find one eating jellyfish at Pulau Redang.

INDONESIA

Diving with *Mola mola* off Bali

Stephen Wong and Takako Uno

Among the 13,670 islands that make up Indonesia, beautiful Bali – 'the Island of Gods' – stands out; Prime Minister Jawaharlal Nehru of India called it 'The morning of the world' when he visited the island during the 1950s. It is home to a rich melting pot of Malay, Chinese, European and Polynesian cultures and has two main religions, Hinduism and Islam.

As if mirroring the cosmopolitan nature of the island's peoples, the waters around Bali teem with life – from rigid stony corals to multi-hued soft corals, from pelagic giants to strange little creatures. Diving in Bali is like reading an encyclopaedia with a kaleidoscope – it is so rich in information, colours and shapes.

But the water does get cold! It had dropped to 16°C (61°F), and I could not believe that this was Bali in August. At 27m (89ft) I could clearly see an upwelling caused by the blending of the water at a thermocline. My fingers and toes were already numb with cold, and in a compressed, five-year-old 5mm (3/16in) wetsuit, or whatever thickness

remained, I had to ascend to a shallower depth before my bare head froze. Then, while signalling to my dive master that I was very cold, I saw my wife, Takako, waving and pointing excitedly. Without any idea of what she was pointing at, I focused in her direction and made out a dark shadow, which took the form of an odd-shaped creature – an Ocean Sunfish!

The visibility was about 25m (75ft) and the sunfish, about 2m (6ft) from fin tip to fin tip, approached us by wagging its dorsal and ventral fins. We had a group of 15 divers, and the funky-looking fish was simply oblivious of our bubbles. It closed to within about 3m (10ft) and investigated the clumsy divers. After satisfying its curiosity, it turned about and swam away in the direction from which it had originally appeared.

A few of us attempted to chase it, but despite its ungainly appearance, it just blended back into the blue at amazing speed.

Following our dive master, we continued along the sloping reef. The dive plan had been to start off from the shallow sandy bottom inside Crystal Bay, proceed to the drop-off and swim along the wall. We would then go around a large pinnacle and end the dive on the other side of the bay, while steering clear of surfacing in blue water above the deep channel.

Everything was going exactly as planned, the experience being enhanced by the fact that our minds were captivated by the sunfish encounter.

Surprisingly, even at this cold and heavily trafficked dive site, the corals were healthy and teeming with multi-coloured Anthias. Resident sweetlips and hubcap-sized Six-banded Angelfish were bold and did not shy away from divers.

My buddy Tommy was having equalization problems with his ears, so he stayed a bit

Opposite *Despite their weird shape, Ocean Sunfish can move faster than divers when they want to.*

Left *A diver videoing an Ocean Sunfish; as always, ethical diving demands that the animal not be disturbed.*

shallower and was leading the rest of us. Then I saw him easing up onto this large shape that resembled a small seamount.

The dive master signalled the divers to stop advancing and beckoned to those with cameras. Tommy, already had his video lights on and as I slowly approached I realized that the seamount was actually alive – it was a mottled behemoth of a sunfish over 3m (10ft) long that dwarfed Tommy – 1.8m (6ft) of him, dangling fins and all.

With an entourage of cleaning Bannerfish, it tilted its large head upward and remained motionless. While opening its comical mouth and rolling its saucer-sized eyes to check us out, it occasionally flapped its tiny pectoral fins to stabilize itself as it enjoyed being cleaned.

Finally, perhaps intimidated as more divers approached it, it decided to leave and vanished even faster than the first had.

Over the next few days we made return visits to Crystal Bay, and checked out other sites in Nusa Lembongan and Nusa Penida. Although a few sunfish were seen at these sites, all of them were at 30–40m (100–130ft).

On one dive I saw two hanging out together. My heart pounded as I approached them, and I was totally oblivious to the sounds from the cracking crustaceans or the dive master's signalling device or even my own breathing. I checked the gauges: I had plenty of air left, but the depth was registering 44m (144ft) and the water was 15°C (60°F). It was no wonder I felt a bit nauseous and light-headed.

The two giants became spooked, veered off a little, but were still within reach. This was tempting, but I had to give up; no picture is worth one's life. Besides, I had seen a handful of sunfish at shallower depths a few days earlier. Waving goodbye to the pair, I started to ascend, hoping to see more of Bali's sunfish another day.

Right *An Ocean Sunfish, perhaps one of the oddest shapes in the ocean, stares into the camera.*

SANGALAKI

Among the best of Indonesian diving

Jack Jackson

Although not the easiest of destinations to reach, the thriving pristine reefs of the islands in the Celebes Sea off Berau on Kalimantan's east coast are certainly among the best of Indonesian diving.

The Island of Sangalaki and its surrounding reefs are protected as an Indonesian Marine Park. The main dive sites are around Pulau Derawan, Pulau Maratua, Pulau Samama, Pulau Kakaban and Pulau Sangalaki with pelagic species being particularly abundant at Pulau Maratua, Pulau

Kakaban and Pulau Sangalaki. You can expect to see shoals of tuna, barracuda, Eagle Rays, Manta Rays, turtles and Scalloped Hammerhead Sharks. Pulau Sangalaki is particularly known for its inquisitive Manta Rays, some of which have wingspans exceeding 5m (16ft). Others are unusual in being totally black.

Located 2° north of the equator and covering 12ha (30 acres) in the Celebes Sea, Sangalaki is covered in dense tropical forest surrounded by white, sandy beaches, perfect for turtles laying eggs. The resort at Pulau Sangalaki was developed by Borneo Divers, but ex-Borneo Divers Director Ron Holland has now taken over on his own under the name Sangalaki Dive Lodge.

There is a tidal range of 2m (6.5ft) at Pulau Sangalaki and the reefs extend out 600–1000m (1970–3280ft), continuing as gentle slopes. A small boat channel is cut through the outer reef and all diving is drift diving from small boats. If diving when the tide is in, divers can board the dive boat at the beach, but by the time they return the dive boat will ground some 150m (500ft) from shore, leaving everyone to walk in. Similarly everyone will have to walk out to the boat for the next dive, but by the time

Opposite *A diver struggles to keep up with a Manta Ray; it's able to move rapidly when it wishes to do so.* **Below** *The spots of a Spotted Eagle Ray show up clearly; these rays feed on molluscs and crustaceans.*

the boat returns the tide will allow the boat right up to the main beach again. Resort staff help divers to carry their equipment.

Two competing resorts have now been set up in the area. One of these is 50 minutes north-northwest on the larger, inhabited island of Pulau Derawan, which has fresh water. Diving at Pulau Derawan is similar to that on Pulau Mabul in eastern Sabah and particularly good for macro photography. During the day, most divers concentrate on Pulau Sangalaki, Pulau Kakaban, Pulau Maratua and Pulau Samama.

The newest resort is Nabucco Island Resort inside Pulau Maratua Lagoon. Maratua is approximately 4km (2.5 miles) long and the northern half of the lagoon rises out of the water; this part is inhabited. It takes an hour or so to get round Pulau Maratua to reach Pulau Sangalaki and Pulau Kakaban in good weather.

The visibility in this area is affected when heavy rain on the mainland increases the river

runoff, but Pulau Sangalaki usually has better visibility than Pulau Samama or Pulau Derawan because it is further offshore. Pulau Kakaban and Pulau Maratua tend to have better visibility than Sangalaki because they are even further out. The lagoon at Pulau Maratua is 100–400m (330–1300ft) wide and is open to the sea via a single channel, creating a very strong tidal flow. This produces amazing drift dives twice a day as the tides race in and out. The pelagic life is prolific, including Scalloped Hammerhead Sharks, Manta and Eagle Rays and, on rare occasions, Whale Sharks. The currents can be really strong and up- and down-currents are common. Most dive operators put divers into the water only on a flood tide. This is because apart from the lower visibility on an ebb tide, they would not want divers being swept out into the open sea where they would be difficult to see.

As an ex-boat skipper, I would advise drift-divers not to wear black or blue buoyancy

control devices (BCDs), which are difficult to see, and they should carry high-visibility surface marker buoys (SMBs) or rescue sausages.

Some 15 minutes northwest of Pulau Sangalaki, Pulau Samama has mangroves open to the sea so the water around the tangled root system is much clearer than you would expect, giving access to the interesting small creatures that inhabit them. About 20–25 minutes east-northeast of Pulau Sangalaki, Pulau Kakaban rises steeply with walls to 240m (790ft) and many pelagic species. These current-swept walls, decorated with gorgonias, soft corals and twisted barrel sponges, give high-voltage drift dives. The currents can be strong with upwelling and downwelling and sometimes they reverse direction but they produce prolific fish life. At Barracuda Point (the southwest point of the island) these currents bring large shoals of barracuda, surgeonfish, snappers, trevallies and Scalloped Hammerhead Sharks.

Pulau Sangalaki is known for its Manta Rays and turtles. A shallow lagoon surrounds the island and the reefs begin well out to

sea. With so much shallow reef, there is a large diversity of marine life and since the area is a protected marine park, the reefs are in good condition. The reefs slope gently with many of the dive sites having a maximum depth of less than 20m (65ft). On almost every dive there are Manta Rays, cuttlefish, Eagle Rays, stingrays, batfish, barracuda, many species of grouper.

The currents vary from medium to strong and these, and the direction in which divers drift, will depend on the direction of the tide at the time of the dive. Snorkelling is the best way to interact with the Manta Rays which then keep on coming back out of curiosity.

At the Southwest corner of the reef, Turtle Patch has turtles sheltering under overhangs formed by large boulder corals at 12m (40ft), and Turtle Town has gullies and small ridges on stony coral in all directions with lots of turtles at 15m (50ft).

At the northwest to west area of the reef, the drift from Manta Run to Sandy Ridge is over undulating sand with coral heads at 28m (92ft), where more than 20 Manta Rays repeatedly swim closely overhead. Manta Parade, the northernmost area of the reef, has a flat sandy bottom, interspersed with small coral heads at 15m (50ft) where Manta Rays parade up and down.

The sun goes out like a light when large Manta Rays pass overhead. In this instance it was a group of five that 'flew' over us. The initial group soon became nine, then 13, 15, 17... and I gave up counting at 20. We were strung out on an old anchor rope at 12m (40ft). Still attached to its anchor, the rope enabled us to hold in the current without damaging any coral. There

were garden eels on a sand patch beside us, but it was the rays that held our attention. Gradually they became more inquisitive, descending from the surface to glide past us in all directions. We remained fairly still and they returned again and again.

Finally our diminishing air supplies forced us to break off the encounter and ascend to the chase boat, but we were then able to join the animals on snorkel. Returning to the beach we found Green Turtle hatchlings fighting their

way out of the sand and heading for the sea. This was just the first of many such encounters at Pulau Sangalaki.

On every dive we encountered Manta Rays and cuttlefish – often laying eggs, and Green and Hawksbill Turtles. If anything, there were more Green Turtles here than at Pulau Sipadan and on average they were larger, particularly the males. Almost every night, light sleepers had their sleep interrupted by turtles nesting outside their accommodation.

THE PHILIPPINES

A world hotspot for Megamouth sightings

Jack Jackson

As with its neighbours Indonesia and Malaysia, the Philippines forms part of the 'Coral or Golden Triangle', composed of the Philippines, Indonesia and Papua New Guinea, and scientists consider that this area has more species of corals, sponges, invertebrates and fish than anywhere else. The Philippines is well known for smaller, reef species and colourful gorgonias, but in addition it has almost all of the pelagic species known to inhabit or pass through warm waters. Some reefs in deep water, such as Apo Reef off Mindoro, the Tubbataha Reefs, Jessie Beazley Reef, Basterra (Mæander) Reef, and the Cagayan Islands – that are well off shore – are either protected, remote or both. Add what is often a strong current and you have ideal conditions for both small and large pelagic species.

Whales, dolphins and pelagic sharks are abundant, and Manta Rays are common on off-shore reefs. However, where the Philippines really stands out, is in the number of Whale Sharks you may encounter and rare Megamouth Sharks.

Whales and dolphins

At least 23 species of whales and dolphins reside in or pass through these waters. Whales include Blainville's Beaked, Bryde's, Fin, Humpback, Sperm, Pygmy Sperm, Dwarf Sperm and Cuvier's Beaked. Dolphins include Rough-toothed, Common Bottlenose, Pan-tropical Spotted, Spinner, Striped, Fraser's and Risso's. You can also encounter other whale species such as Melon-headed, Pygmy Killer, False Killer, Killer and Shortfin Pilot. Irrawaddy Dolphins and Finless Porpoises may be found, as might further species of cetaceans including Minke and Blue Whales.

Dolphins frequent all waters in the Philippines but are more likely to be encountered when travelling to or from reefs or islands. In my own experience, it is almost impossible to travel by boat or ship anywhere in the Sulu Sea in daylight without dolphins being continuously in view.

Opposite The largest fish in the ocean, majestic Whale Sharks are easily recognized by their pattern of spots.
Above A Fin Whale approaching the surface to blow; they dive to depths of 200m (660ft).
Below Striped Dolphins are often seen surfing in large groups. This species is easily recognized by the stripe that runs from its dark coloured rostrum, around the eye, and down along the side to the rear flank

Whale Sharks

Today, Whale Sharks could be called common in parts of the Philippines. However, before hunting them was banned in 1998 and the hunters were encouraged to run Whale Shark tours instead, the animals had been caught traditionally with spears and gaffs from small boats in the Visayas and Mindanao regions. The six-man crews often caught four in a day.

Then, in late 1997 it was discovered that a concentration of Whale Sharks had been visiting the mouth of Donsol River for many generations; they had not previously been fished in this area, which is part of the Bicol region of southern Luzon. In fact, there were so many of them that a dozen or more could be encountered in a single day without the use of spotter planes. The animals were monitored by

the World Wildlife Fund-Philippines, in association with Silliman University, Hubbs-SeaWorld Research Institute, Scripps Institution of Oceanography, the US National Oceanographic and Atmospheric Administration, and the Philippines Department of Agriculture. The local authorities at Donsol issued a resolution to protect the sharks and to develop ecotourism involving Whale Shark interaction tours.

However, the news of the find unfortunately attracted buyers of Whale Sharks from the Visayas region and seven sharks were killed and sold for export under licence to Taiwan. This caused nationwide alarm and WWF-Philippines immediately expressed concern that the population could be eradicated. They requested a moratorium on the fishery and trade in Bicol until sufficient data could be

gathered on the concentration's population size, movement and sustainable use.

The news of the kill – including bloody pictures of the animals being butchered – soon reached the national press. Conservationists were incensed. As a result of lobbying, on 26 March 1998, Fisheries Administrative Order No. 193 was issued prohibiting the capture, sale, purchase and possession, transport and export of Whale Sharks throughout the Philippines. In addition, this order also covered Manta Rays, which had been fished in large numbers in the Visayas and Mindanao.

Organized Whale Shark expeditions, which included swimming with the 'Butanding', the local name for the animal, transformed the sleepy, fishing village of Donsol into a major ecotourism destination almost overnight. Today

Above Adult Great Hammerhead Sharks are larger than other hammerheads and are easily distinguished by their tall first dorsal fin.

Left Blacktip Sharks are often found on nearshore reefs and near estuaries but not in fresh water.

it is known as the Whale Shark capital of the world. Small boats now take the tourists to see the animals between January and May. The animals arrive in January, numbers peak in March and April and towards the end of May, and then dwindle again.

In June when the rains arrive, the weather deteriorates, the sea becomes choppy and Donsol and the surrounding area doze for a few months until the weather improves again.

The animals can be anywhere, but it's a large area of sea so there is never any guarantee of success. However, in January 2005, Time Magazine identified the Philippines' WWF-supported Whale Shark interaction programme off the Donsol River as the 'Best Place for an Animal Encounter'. Local fishermen have

become tour-boat operators, and others have been trained as spotters to scan the water for the slowly moving shadows and fins. Most tourists prefer to remain on deck, but others slip quietly into the water to get a close view. Disturbance is minimized: only snorkelling is permitted, flash photography is not allowed and a code of conduct prevents tourists from touching the animals.

'These filter-feeders are attracted by the abundance of zooplankton, small fish, squid, and crustaceans in the waters of Donsol,' said Ruel Pine, WWF-Philippines' Community-based Ecotourism and Coastal Resource Management project manager.

'Based on tours made in 2004, one can sight as many as 30 Whale Sharks a day,' he adds. The maximum ever reported is 57. The only problem is that the plankton can be so thick that getting a good photograph is rare.

WWF-Philippines, together with Donsol's local government, police, women's groups and fishing communities, has established the Task Force Sagip Kalikasan (TFSK), which

Left Oceanic Whitetip Sharks are among the most impressive of sharks, they are easily recognized by their long, paddle-like pectoral fins.

Below left Pelagic Thresher Sharks are often found near offshore coral reefs and seamounts.

Opposite Rarely seen, the plankton-feeding Megamouth Sharks have huge mouths that extend behind the eyes.

regularly monitors the municipal waters, particularly against illegal fishing.

'The Whale Shark ecotourism programme is a testimony to the importance of a successful multi-stakeholder involvement,' says Pine.

Despite its 'world capital' appellation, Donsol is only one of many good areas for sighting Whale Sharks in Philippines' waters. There are many good spots but Bohol and Southern Leyte are particularly good.

The name Pamilacan Island is derived from the word pilak, which is a large hooked implement made and used by the islanders to hunt Bryde's Whales, Whale Sharks, dolphins and Manta Rays for as long as their grandparents can remember.

There was initial opposition to stopping this hunt but a US$150,000 grant from a US bank helped in the provision of another source of income for those involved. They now boast of having these former hunters as guides and spotters for up to 100 tourists per day. Some operators from nearby Bohol Island also run their own whale-watching tours.

Divers off Moalboal are now seeing more and more Whale Sharks. There were nearly 50 sightings in 2004, and already, at the time of writing, in January 2005 alone there have been 19 reported sightings, most of them being on the house reef.

Waters off Dumaguete, Busuanga and Coron, and Southern Leyte, especially around Sogod Bay where they were hunted long ago and the children regularly rode on their backs, all have good sightings of Whale Sharks.

Sharks

The chances of spotting the larger predatory sharks in Southeast Asia are not good unless divers are at more remote areas near deep water. The sharks are still around the shallower reefs, but not in large numbers due to overfishing. In the Philippines, Scalloped Hammerheads and Pelagic Thresher Sharks are relatively common at reefs near deep water. However, your chances of seeing most of the other species are best at the more remote, protected reefs such as Apo Reef off Mindoro and Tubbataha Reef, Jessie Beazley Reef, Basterra (Mæander) Reef, and the Cagayan Islands, and other reefs in the Sulu Sea.

Pelagic species to be found in these waters include Blacktip, Blue, Bull, Dusky, Oceanic Whitetip, Pelagic Thresher, Great Hammerhead, Scalloped Hammerhead, Megamouth, Shortfin Mako, Silky, Silvertip and Tiger.

In recent years, divers have descended *en masse* to Malapascua where a Pelagic Thresher Shark cleaning station had been found at Monad Shoal. The sharks are still there but diver numbers and fishermen have taken their toll so you are much less likely to get close to the sharks nowadays.

Scalloped Hammerhead Sharks and threshers are seen almost everywhere there is deep water but they rarely get close enough to be photographed. At Puerto Galera, Scalloped Hammerheads and threshers are being seen above the Canyons. At Boracay, Scalloped Hammerheads are seen at Yapak 1 and 2 and at Cabilao Island, shoals of Scalloped Hammerheads are found at Lighthouse Wall

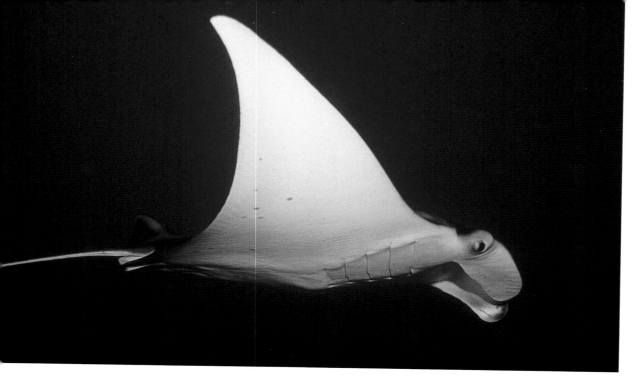

Above When feeding, Manta Rays extend horn-like flaps to channel plankton into their mouths.

Opposite Green Turtles will allow divers to get close if they approach quietly; I have even had them fall asleep in front of me.

and Hammerhead Point. Pescador Island sees shoals of Scalloped Hammerheads and Malapascua has thresher and Silvertip Sharks at Monad Shoal. While all the big sharks are found at Apo Reef off Mindoro and Tubbataha Reefs, Jessie Beazley Reef, and other remote reefs in the Sulu Sea, Oceanic Whitetip, Blue, thresher and Shortfin Makos are mostly found in open water off reefs in deep water. Bull Sharks are more likely to be seen near river outlets while Tiger Sharks can be seen anywhere, especially near ports.

In addition to its Whale Sharks, the Philippines is a hotspot for Megamouths. On 30 January 2005, a 4.17m (14ft) Megamouth was found enmeshed in a fishing net in Barangay Agusan, Mindanao, and it was only the 25th Megamouth Shark captured and killed worldwide. Of the 25 recorded Megamouth findings throughout the world, four have been found in the Philippines. Two were found in Cagayan de Oro, Mindanao – Megamouth 11

on 20 February 1998 and Megamouth 18 on 6 January 2003. Megamouth 24 was found on 4 November 2004 at Iloilo, Panay Island.

From recorded findings of this endangered species, it would seem that Macajalar Bay, Mindanao is important to Megamouths as three of the 25 finds worldwide were in this bay.

Manta Rays

Manta Rays are widespread in Philippines waters in shallow or deep water. They are particularly common anywhere that you find Whale Sharks, and at Apo Reef off Mindoro and the Tubbataha Reefs and other reefs in the Sulu Sea. The reefs at Tubbataha have a good mixture of juvenile Manta Rays staying over the coral and adults cruising along the walls.

They are abundant from Donsol to the Ticao Pass, the body of water between the main island and Ticao Island. At one site here, Manta Bowl – a depression in a shallow part of Ticao Pass – groups of 15 Manta Rays have been seen feeding.

Some other good places to see Manta Rays include Apo Reef off Mindoro, Apo Island off Negros, Pamilacan Island, Monad Shoal at Malapascua, Moalboal, Siquijor Island, Malaroroy Island, Sogod Bay, El Nido, Lo-oc Bay, and The Canyons at Puerto Galera.

Marine turtles

Marine turtles are living fossils, virtually unchanged, that have roamed the tropical seas for 130 million years. Unfortunately, they are also among the most endangered animals. They are hunted for their meat and to be turned into marine curios.

To exacerbate the situation, their eggs are taken for food and because they are known to mate for up to two hours, their eggs are thought to be an aphrodisiac. This is not borne out scientifically as they are less nutritional than hens' eggs. In addition, their nesting sites are taken over for development. They are crushed by dredgers, run over by pleasure boats, poisoned by pollution, starved when ingesting plastic bags and drowned by fishing lines and nets. As a result, all species of marine turtles are listed as endangered.

Five species of marine turtles are known to occur in the Philippines: Green, Hawksbill, Olive Ridley, Loggerhead and Leatherback.

The Philippines shares a group of nine islands known as the Turtle Islands with Malaysia. The group, which straddles the border with Malaysia, used to be a weekend destination for the British, and residents of the old part of North Borneo that is now Sabah. The Philippines owns six of the islands in the group – Baguan, Taganak, Lihiman, Boan, Langaan and the Great Bakkungan, and Malaysia owns the other three – Pulau Gulisan, Pulau Selingan, and Pulau Bakkungan Kecil. These islands are situated at the southwestern tip of the Philippines, about 1000km (620 miles) southwest of Manila, south of Palawan, northwest of Tawi-Tawi, and northeast of Sabah in Malaysia.

Using satellite telemetry from the uninhabited island of Baguan, scientists track the movements of Green and Hawksbill Turtles, but although this cross-border protected area is Southeast Asia's single most important Green Turtle conservation area, not all of the turtles encountered in the Philippines are found here. The most abundant turtle in the Philippines is the Green Turtle, which got its English name from its green fat produced by its diet of sea-grass. These turtles have been seen as far north as Fuga Island in Cagayan, and south, off Bancoran, Palawan. Because of their tasty meat, they are also the most threatened.

Considered the most beautiful of all sea turtles, Hawksbills feed mainly on sponges. Quite small, they got their English name from

their hawk-like beak, that is used to pick small animals from coral reefs. This species inhabits the Celebes Sea, the Cuyo island group of Palawan, Jolo, Cotabato, and Sitangkai in Tawi-Tawi, Sablayan in Occidental Mindoro and the open waters of Sulu Sea.

Although rarely seen in the Philippines, the Leatherback Turtle got its English name from its leathery back; it feeds primarily on jellyfish and roams the open seas. The Olive Ridley Turtle has been seen by fisher-

men in the shallow, coastal waters of Paluan, Occidental Mindoro. The Logger-head is a large-headed turtle that feeds in estuaries and along the continental shelf, using its strong jaw muscles to crush molluscs and crustaceans.

I have encountered Green and Hawks-bill Turtles in most of their domains in the Philippines, but, as a result of illegal hunting, they are most likely to be found in protected or little-inhabited areas.

Above *A lucky photographer gets close to a Manta Ray hovering at the reef to be cleaned.*

Greater Pacific

PAPUA NEW GUINEA

The Manta Rays of Milne Bay

Bob Halstead

From my earliest dives in Milne Bay Province, Papua New Guinea, in 1973, I can still remember thrilling encounters with Manta Rays. Unfortunately these wonderful dives could not be predicted. It seemed all a matter of luck – and that seemed to be mostly bad luck, as I inevitably would have a close-up lens on my camera when the manta appeared.

My bad luck continued in the early 1980s when a pod of Killer Whales appeared at East Cape, at the northeastern entrance to Milne Bay, and set about eating all the mantas in that area. In 1998 aboard Golden Dawn I set out with Captain Craig de Wit to find where we could take divers and guarantee them mantas. He can trace his ancestors back to a rapacious Dutch pirate and there is no doubt that Craig has inherited his adventurous spirit. We didn't seize any other vessels on our cruise but I did notice a gleam in Craig's eye when a particularly well-laden cargo vessel steamed past.

I love exploration diving and as the sun rose over the calm sea I rejoiced in a few glorious moments alone on the top deck, contemplating and relishing the day ahead.

There was no sign of mantas at the first two sites and so we cruised to a third near a village. The news was good. Villagers of Gonubalabala Island told us that there were always mantas about, and when the tide changed they would come close to the island. So, we anchored and started to send divers off in different directions to explore the reef. Some dived directly from the *Golden Dawn* while others took off in the inflatable.

Large coral boulders, carpeted by a healthy cover of soft corals, were scattered over the sandy bottom, with big sweetlips and groupers peering out from ledges beneath them. Suddenly an enormous school of Bumphead Parrotfish appeared – and just as quickly took off again as they realized that there were strangers in their realm. It was obvious that this reef had not been dived before. Visibility was modest since the water was loaded with plankton, but this is just what Manta Rays feed on.

I surfaced to find that mantas had been seen feeding on the surface on the other side of the island so I raced off with a couple of others to see if we could snorkel with them. Sure enough at least a dozen dark shapes moved just below the surface with an occasional dorsal fin or wingtip slicing into the air. I soon had some pictures of the magnificent fish as they passed me, mouths agape and feeding, and barely reacting to my presence. These pelagic mantas were in deep water and I hung on to my camera with a firm grip, wishing that I had thought of a neck strap. If I let it slip here it

would be gone forever. On the way back to the boat we saw Craig waving to us and a marker float nearby. He was raving about giant mantas being cleaned at a rock he had found in just 9m (30ft) of water. So I went back in and snorkelled over to the rock following Craig's directions from his marker. I looked down to see two really big mantas just hovering near the rock as cleaner fish tended them. Evidently they were taking turns to come in from the deep to be cleaned. I quietly dived down and glided towards them, the mantas allowed me to get some close photographs before they slowly swam off to continue feeding.

Craig took my tank for a quick refill while I snorkelled, and on his return I quickly donned it, went down to the rock by myself and huddled close against it, breathing quietly and hoping for the mantas' return.

Only a minute went by before two arrived. I held my breath as one stopped right over my head only centimetres away and filled

the frame of my super-wide 16mm fisheye lens. An hour later others joined me in this close encounter of the miraculous kind so I surfaced to reload my camera.

It was one of the great dives of my life. Never had I been able to get so close to mantas and have them aware of, and welcoming, my presence. We had been eyeball to eyeball.

I felt that they actually liked me.

Craig scheduled divers in small groups on the cleaning bommie (coral head) throughout the rest of the day. Being so shallow there was never any problem with bottom times, we just carried on diving. Sometimes the mantas were absent for up to half an hour but everyone in the group was able to see them close up at some time during the day at the rock, and snorkel with them feeding on the surface or in deeper water.

It was fascinating being able to admire the superb grace and control of these magnificent creatures. When hovering, the mantas gently flap the ends of their wings to hold position.

Right *Open wide! A hovering manta is cleaned by wrasse and remoras.*

Opposite *Waiting quietly on the bottom, this diver is having a thrilling close encounter with a manta; the cleaning rock is in the background.*

Once I was so close I was sure the manta would hit me but it just lifted its wing to slowly glide by, barely a centimetre above my head. They seemed to enjoy our visits and would sometimes swim over to divers sitting on the sand near the bommie.

Mantas do not welcome riders, or clumsy grabs, and you should not touch them anyway. But they are often quite happy to get very close; patient divers who stay still on the bottom are often rewarded by a manta gently descending right on top of them appearing to enjoy a gentle massage from the diver's exhaust bubbles.

The manta dive site, which Craig named 'Giants At Home' is now one of Milne Bay Province's most popular. The villagers at Gonubalabala Island protect the mantas and keep a logbook of visiting boats, which are encouraged to report encounters.

Up to nine of the creatures have been reported at the rock at any one time with more

Above *Mantas on their daily parade past the beach and fringing reef at Gonubalabala Island.*

Right *An enormous 'Darth Vader', as we call the awesome black mantas, is joined by a smaller manta in a soaring ballet at the cleaning rock. Individual mantas are easily distinguished by the black and white patterns on their underside.*

swimming on the surface nearby. The usual procedure is to place a small marker float in the shallows by the beach then run a line along the seabed to the cleaning station. This prevents the possibility of mantas getting tangled in lines at the site. Boats anchor over a patch of sand a short swim away.

Mantas are usually at the main cleaning station but they are also attracted to a few supplementary stations in the area. Other creatures often seen are Dugongs, Wobbegong Sharks, stingrays, and a large array of muck

diving creatures such as Blue-ringed Octopuses, sea horses, nudibranchs and frogfish.

Papua New Guinea is blessed by visits from many pelagics. For example, whales of various species may be seen, particularly in Kimbe Bay and the Bali Vitu group; Whale Sharks migrate

annually along the north coast from Lae to Milne Bay and Port Moresby, and sharks, particularly Silvertips and Scalloped Hammerheads, are still regularly reported. Even Raggedtooth Sharks (also known as Sand Tiger or Grey Nurse Sharks), more often associated with cooler temperate waters, may be encountered at a depth of 40m (130ft) or more, cruising near deep walls.

'Giants At Home' is special because of its remarkable reliability – only once in 100 dives have the mantas failed to show for us. Timing and tides are important with a preference for some current at the rock, which helps the mantas hover, but given this, a superb close and personal dive with one of nature's most impressive pelagic giants can be expected.

FIJI
The home of 'Ratu Rua' – Big Boss Fish

Doug Perrine

When eight species of sharks, five of which are dangerous to humans, compete with other fish for food, which one is dominant? The answer at Shark Reef in Fiji's Beqa Passage, Viti Levu Island, is simple... none – because Ratu Rua, a colossal Giant Grouper, dominates everything else that swims. 'Ratu' is a Fijian title for nobility, and it is clear that the other fish respect the status of this royal when it appears out of the blue with its entourage of Golden Trevallies. Ratu Rua will chase even 3m (10ft) Bull Sharks out of the way when it wants to feed. Once it has gulped a mouthful, though, it retreats to the background, and the sharks are left to compete with each other and with the Giant Trevallies, which easily dominate the smaller sharks.

The operator, who has an exclusive licence to stage feeds at Shark Reef, does not call this a shark dive, but rather a 'Big Fish Encounter'. Pelagic creatures, by their nature, cannot be guaranteed to show up at any given location, even when massive amounts of food are offered as bait. Usually divers see several species of sharks, and sometimes up to eight on a single dive, but the only thing that is promised is that there will be big fish, including several kinds of pelagics, such as Giant Trevallies and Rainbow Runners.

The Giant Trevallies are very impressive and absolutely fearless. Dive masters consider them the most dangerous fish on the reef, and can illustrate their point with assorted body scars. The trevallies turn black while in feeding mode, and zoom into the fray like stealth fighters. Even the reef fish have attained immense proportions

Opposite Befitting royalty, 'Ratu Rua' arrives with an entourage of juvenile Golden Trevally pilot fish.
Right Giant Trevally have strong jaws and move fast. It's advisable to wear dark gloves and watch your fingers when feeding is happening!
Below Manasa hands off a chunk of fish to the Silvertip Shark known as 'Madonna'.

here. A scene-stealing 1.5m (5ft) Humphead (Napoleon) Wrasse easily pushes through clouds of 10kg (22lb) Red Snappers to reach the bait.

Feeding fish, especially sharks, is controversial, but the operator here is not apologetic. Says co-owner Mike Neumann: 'We call it a show. We don't call it an eco-dive.' His rationale is that giving living sharks an economic value is the only way to stop them being slaughtered for their flesh and fins. As proof of the validity of this approach, he points to the newly created Shark Reef Marine Reserve, patrolled by volunteer wardens from the two villages, which share traditional ownership of this reef. Both villages receive payments from fees collected from each diver entering the reserve.

As for having his staff hand-feed the sharks, Neumann says 'Some people may say this is a circus, and it's true – it is a circus. But it is the only way to pay for the marine reserve.' The operator also supports scientific research on the

sharks here. The fish-feed creates a totally unnatural situation on the reef, but it's hard to argue that the ecosystem has been damaged.

Shark Reef was chosen for the dive because it was already over-fished and over-collected, and large areas of the reef slope consisted of dead coral rubble – not susceptible to damage by the shark divers kneeling on it. The addition of copious amounts of natural fish parts bought from a fish processor seems to have actually increased the biodiversity. Nearly 300 species of fish have been counted there recently, while very few fish were seen before the feeding began.

Hand-feeding sharks is not only unnatural, but inherently dangerous. However, the dive is set up so that the risk to guests is minimal, while the feeders themselves have three types of protection.

The most important of all is their intimate knowledge of every shark that visits the reef. It has been gained over the course of hundreds of dives as the same feeders have been staging the show since the dive was started in 1999.

In addition, they are also protected by Fijian magic. They come from a small island whose residents have a traditional non-aggression pact with sharks. Men from this island never harm sharks, and in turn are not harmed by them. Incidentally, their magic also protects them from injury when they walk across hot coals, a

traditional ceremony, which is more frequently performed for tourists these days.

The protection they rely on least is the chain-mail butcher's-glove that covers the feeding hand, although this provides an excellent shield against nips by Giant Trevallies.

The encounter is staged as a two-tank multi-level dive. The first starts at 30m (100ft), where guests kneel behind a low stone wall at the edge of the reef slope. On the other side of the wall, the feeders pull big hunks of fish out of a large garbage bin and offer it to sharks that swim in.

Beefy Bull Sharks are the main attraction, although Sharptooth Lemon and Silvertip Sharks are regular visitors as well. After about 15 minutes

Above At the Shark Reef Marine Reserve, Hamilton the Humphead (Napoleon) Wrasse is safe from the Hong Kong restaurant trade.

Opposite top Scalloped Hammerhead Sharks are typically found on deep pinnacles and drop-offs near open ocean.

Opposite below Rusi holds a snack for the Tiger Shark known as 'Scarface', a semi-regular visitor.

the divers move up the slope to a depth of about 14m (45ft) to finish the dive. The dive masters usually concentrate on drawing out moray eels and other reef fish during this part of the dive.

The second dive takes place at the same 14m (45ft) spot on the slope.

Here the guests line up behind a rope, while the feeders work on the other side, slightly down-slope. The Bull and Silvertip Sharks often ascend for the second feed and join reef sharks that are found at this depth. About once a week, a Tiger Shark arrives; larger Tigers make even the brawny Bull Sharks look like minnows.

There are other shark encounters in Fiji, but these generally only involve reef sharks — no pelagic species. However, with over 300 islands spread across a huge expanse of ocean, there are plenty of opportunities for pelagic encounters.

Manta Rays are regularly encountered at Manta Reef, near Kadavu on the Great Astrolabe Reef. Other sites near Kadavu feature shoals of Eagle Rays and barracuda.

Wakaya Island, east of Viti Levu Island, offers frequent sightings of Manta Rays and hammerhead sharks. At nearby Namena Marine Reserve, off the southwest corner of Vanua Levu Island, there is a site called Grand Central Station, known for sightings of pelagics, including Manta Rays, Mobula Rays, pilot whales, Dogtooth Tuna, schooling barracuda, mackerel, trevallies, and Rainbow Runners.

Namena is the only place in Fiji where a Humpback Whale is known to have given birth. Humpbacks also pass the island of Taveuni in July during their annual migration while Spinner Dolphins can be found year-round in several areas, including Namoto Island in the Mamanuca Islands, and Sperm Whales can sometimes be encountered in the deep waters off the Lau Group.

The 'pelagic potential' of this island nation is probably only just beginning to be realized.

FRENCH POLYNESIA

Where you can swim with Humpback Whales

By Lawson Wood

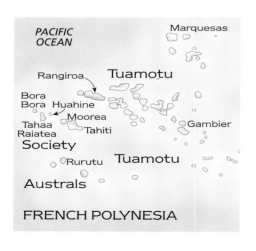

French Polynesia... what an opportunity! I had always wanted to go to the South Pacific. Idle thoughts of sun-kissed beaches – or was that sun-kissed maidens? – flitted across my mind.

But hang on... isn't French Polynesia simply massive? I mean, doesn't it cover an area the size of Europe and have a choice of literally hundreds of islands? Where do you go when you get there? With whom do you dive? What is there to see that makes it so special? Why go to Polynesia instead of anywhere else in the general area? A quick look on the Internet, and I had the answers. There were all those images I had dreamed about earlier, and so much more. There were stories of shoals of sharks, amazing wall diving, regular sightings of dolphins, sharks, Manta Rays. Did I mention sharks? And even whales! Not to mention sun-kissed maidens, black pearls and indeed some of the most scenically beautiful islands I have ever seen anywhere.

There are actually five archipelagos comprising 118 islands and more atolls than you can shake a snorkel at. At the extreme north are the Marquesas, made famous by the writings of Herman Melville and by French artist Paul Gauguin. The low-lying Tuomotas, once referred to as the 'dangerous islands', are to the west and boast some of the finest coral atolls in the world.

The Gambier Archipelago to the east is more rugged, but has even more atolls, which are famous for their pearl farms.

The Society Islands, which comprise the Windward and Leeward Islands to the south-west, have perhaps what many people believe are the most scenically beautiful of all the island groups. These include Tahiti, Moorea, Taha'a, Raiatea, Huahine and Bora Bora.

The Austral Archipelago lies to the south, with a more temperate environment, cooler waters and poorer visibility. So why would we want to go there? The answer's simple: Rurutu in the Australs is one of the very few locations on the planet where you can swim with Humpback Whales. Astounding!

Top of the list for many divers is visiting the second largest atoll in the world, in the Tuomotas. At over 75km (47 miles) long, Rangiroa, or 'Rangi' as it is called locally, is more like an inland sea; surrounded by tiny islets or 'motu'. For the most part they are uninhabited, save for the thousands of seabirds that have found sanctuary there.

The island communities, comprising Avatoru, Tevaiohie and Reoprepo, are known collectively as Rangiroa. It is flanked on either side by the two channels that feed and cleanse the lagoon twice daily. In particular, Tiputa Pass to the east is incredible. Tiputa was once a river, when Rangiroa was a mountain, millennia ago. It has depths on the ocean side of the pass at over 70m (230ft), rising to 6m (20ft) on the inside of the cut. The island of Rurutu, located far to the south in the Austral archipelago, is tiny and shaped like continental Africa and only

Right A Humpback Whale calf glides gracefully into the depths. Today there are about 30–40,000 Humpback Whales – around a third of their original population.
Top right The small dorsal fin of the Humpback Whale is quite distinctive on the surface.
Opposite Breaching male Humpback Whales posture to each other prior to mating with the females.

10km (6 miles) by 5km (3 miles). The flying time is 90 minutes on the local Air Tahiti thrice-weekly service. More temperate in climate, Rurutu has cooler waters and less visibility than the heady excesses of the northern islands and atolls. This rural backwater now has an unlikely boost to its economy: you are almost guaranteed an encounter with Humpback Whales.

From late August to late November each year females visit Rurutu's waters to give birth and mate. Accompanied by one or two mature males, which are most favoured for mating, and several juvenile opportunistic males (some things never change!), the females congregate in the shallow waters near the reef passes.

Yves Lefevre and Eric Le Borgne of Raie Manta Club run the whale-watching and snorkel encounters. Space is limited as there are only three local boats, piloted by local fishermen. The boats are licensed to each carry six passengers and a guide, to minimize stress to the whales, and they run for about three hours each morning and afternoon. Prior to the encounters, guests are given comprehensive instructions on how to approach the whales safely and with minimal disruption to their routine.

Once a breaching whale is sighted, the boats move to the approximate area while the whale goes through its regular breathing routine of surfacing approximately three times before 'sounding' or diving deep on the fourth breath. This behaviour is clearly recognizable, as it is the only time that the whale lifts its gigantic tail clear of the water.

Once the whale sounds, it can be around 15–18 minutes before it surfaces again. It is this interval that the whale-watchers look for, as this could mean that the whale is having a short rest or sleeping.

The best encounters are with resting or sleeping whales, as they tend to be suspended in water around 15–25m (50–80ft). Snorkellers armed with a multitude of underwater cameras wait on the surface near where they hope that the whale will start to rise towards the surface. It is at this point, when the animal almost reaches the surface, that you are allowed a shallow snorkel dive and the chance to photograph these mighty beasts. But the whole encounter is not as easy as it sounds.

You can spend the entire time in a windy, small, rocking boat, slipping into 21°C (70°F) water perhaps half a dozen times only to find that the whale has moved off. It can also be a bit of a 'bun-fight' as only the strongest swimmer

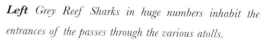

Left Grey Reef Sharks in huge numbers inhabit the entrances of the passes through the various atolls.
Top left Humpback Whales blow gently while resting on the surface.
Opposite After two or three surface breaths, the Humpback Whale lifts its distinctively marked tail before sounding (diving deep).

may have a chance to stay that bit longer with the whale, but you have to get past the phalanx of other underwater photographers, all trying to get the best shot.

In-water encounters are never guaranteed, but there were numerous sightings on the surface as we followed the whales as they moved around the island.

We witnessed full breaching, fluke slapping and tail slapping as well as close inspections of the 40-tonne animals as they swam past the boat with surprising speed. We had perhaps nine sightings while snorkelling on and under the water during four trips. Not exactly fruitful from a photographic point of view, but I have to say that the encounters that we had have more than fuelled this diver's dream of swimming with one of the largest and gentlest animals in the world.

HAWAII

Where you can hear the whales sing

Doug Perrine

Hawaiian Islands

Kauai
Niihau
Oahu
Honolulu
Molokai
Lanai
Maui
Kahoolawe
Hawaii

PACIFIC OCEAN

This time there was no doubt that it was the same one. Usually, when an 8m (25ft) polka-dotted fish bumps up against your boat, it's hard to be sure if it's the same one that did the same thing two days ago. Secondly, when Whale Sharks show up in Hawaii, several may be sighted in the same area in a short time. Lastly, the shock of seeing an animal as long as the boat often excites people beyond the point of making a detailed analysis of the spot-pattern that distinguishes one individual from another. This shark, however, was blue. It was

unquestionably the same one that had spent two hours rubbing the blue paint off the boat's hull earlier in the week. And when the divers grabbed their snorkels and jumped into the water, its behaviour was the same: it tried to rub up against them as well. Hilarious video clips show divers swimming confidently towards the big blue fish, then back-pedalling and frantically thrashing out of the way as the gentle giant turns towards them.

Sightings of Whale Sharks in Hawaiian waters are sporadic and unpredictable, but there is always something interesting swimming around in the vast, boundless realm of Blue Hawaii – the zone beyond where the seafloor can be seen from the surface. In these clear waters that typically means waters deeper than about 30m (100ft). However, the slopes of these volcanic islands are so steep that this featureless expanse of uniform cobalt blue often starts within a stone's throw of the shoreline. That's why some divers on shore dives have sighted sailfish, Manta Rays, Eagle Rays, hammerhead sharks, Humpback Whales and other denizens of the deep. Tiger Sharks and Oceanic Whitetip Sharks have been known to swim into small-boat harbours in Hawaii.

Of course, using a boat greatly improves the odds of pelagic encounters by allowing a larger area of mostly empty ocean to be searched. However, the prevailing trade winds that blow across the state from the northeast complicate this by creating rough conditions on the windward side of the islands, making it hard to spot surface disturbances that signal the presence of an animal just below. Therefore, most pelagic searches are conducted on the lee (western) sides of the islands. Hawaii Island, or the Big Island, with its massive volcanoes, produces the largest wind-shadow on its lee, or Kona, side.

Due to the likelihood of returning with nothing but sunburn, backache and a large fuel bill to show for a day cruising around off shore, full-day pelagic excursions are generally by private charter only.

However, especially in Kona, dive boats often swing off shore during surface intervals, hoping to bump into something interesting.

Right *Sailfish are less common in Hawaiian waters than Blue Marlin, but are occasionally seen – even on shore dives!*

Opposite *Oceanic Whitetips often approach divers closely, and may gradually escalate to bumping. Possibly they are testing defensive capabilities.*

While Whale Sharks, Leatherback Turtles, and other ocean wanderers pass through Hawaiian waters irregularly, other large inhabitants of the deep, blue zone are resident in Hawaiian waters.

Among the most common deep-water residents spotted from the surface are Shortfin Pilot Whales. These travel back and forth off the coastline, feeding on deep-water squid in waters hundreds of metres deep, resting and socializing at the surface between feeding dives. They tend to be sensitive and aloof, and generally avoid interaction with divers. On occasions they can become aggressive.

Pilot whales and other marine mammals are easily disturbed by human activities, and are protected by the US Marine Mammal Protection Act. Other marine mammals are additionally protected by the Endangered Species Act, which carries much larger fines. To avoid interfering with essential activities of wildlife, and to avoid legal problems, divers are

advised to check on protected species before venturing off shore, and to utilize reputable operators with the knowledge and experience to achieve a rewarding experience without harm to either animals or humans. Or getting a fine!

The interest offshore divers have in pilot whales is partly related to the company they keep. For reasons not understood, Oceanic Whitetip Sharks often accompany them.

So, by entering the water just after a pod of pilots has passed, divers can be in an excellent position to be investigated by an Oceanic Whitetip Shark or two.

But you should take care, however: while the author is not aware of any divers in Hawaii being injured by this species, most authorities consider it to be extremely dangerous. It is considered to be responsible for many deaths, particularly following disasters at sea.

Certainly they are very bold and persistent predators/scavengers, and a diver would not

want to be far away from the boat while in the presence of one of these sharks. Nothing this author writes should be taken as encouragement for any one of you to expose yourself to this or any other dangerous sea creature without a cage or other method of protection. Having said that, the fact is cages are rarely used for encounters with Oceanic Whitetip Sharks in Hawaii.

On the other hand, snorkellers are required to stay inside the cage by the operators offering encounters with Sandbar and Galápagos Sharks off Oahu's North Shore. Tourist boats conduct several tours every morning, going out about 5km (3 miles) from shore to an area used by crab-trappers. The trappers discard old bait when they haul in their traps, so the sharks have learned that the sound of a boat arriving in this area means food.

The tourist boats use fish-scraps to draw the sharks close to the surface-floating cages.

Usually sharks come to the boats as soon as they stop, and dozens may be seen.

In the vastness of the open ocean it is rarely easy to locate the few large animals that inhabit this blue wilderness so it is often helpful to look for floating logs, nets, or other debris that can act as attractants. Even a coconut or plastic bucket may have accumulated an entourage beneath it. Larger masses, such as nets, may house Sargassumfish (one of the frog-fish family) and other interesting creatures as well as attracting pelagic fish such as Mahi-Mahi (Dorado or Dolphinfish).

Fish aggregating devices (FADs), which are large spherical buoys moored to the seabed, play an important role in attracting fish. The locations of these devices are published, and can be located by a Global Positioning System (GPS) receiver, but bear in mind their actual position may vary, due to the length of the line required

Above A Spotted Eagle Ray cruises along the reef.
Above left Pilot whales typically retreat to deeper water when they encounter humans.
Opposite Exactly how the Whale Shark's curious polka-dotted colour pattern helps it survive in open blue water is a mystery.

to secure them to the seabed – which may be thousands of metres below.

The powerful ocean currents that shift the FADs around demand respect, and are believed to be the main reason a FAD can be totally devoid of life on one day, but host a circus of feeding tuna, marlin, and sharks on the next. Spear fishers sometimes visit FADs in hopes of landing a large tuna, Mahi-Mahi, or Wahoo, and larger predators such as Oceanic Whitetip Sharks, Roughtooth Dolphins, and False Killer Whales may employ the same strategy. Several blue-water divers have reported having terrified Mahi-Mahi rush in and try to hide under their arms when pursued by False Killer Whales. Others have reported that False Killer Whales approached them with a fish already in the mouth, offering to share it.

But how do Hawaii's clear blue offshore waters, which are mostly devoid of plankton, support healthy populations of game fish, dolphins, and whales? Well, during the day the base of the food chain is out of sight, a few hundred metres below the surface but at night, however, this plankton-rich zone – known as the deep-scattering layer – rises to the surface and some Kona dive boats occasionally run special charters, drifting offshore at night with bright lights and a sea anchor.

The main attraction on these night drifts is in seeing the myriad and bizarre small transparent, drifting organisms, including larval fish and invertebrates, jellies, and salps, plus pelagic squid, octopuses, and sea horses. However, on occasion larger visitors, including a Whale Shark and a Bigeye Thresher Shark, have poked their heads into the pool of light. Kona's most famous night dive is conducted close to shore in about 15m (45ft) of water.

Divers sit on the bottom in a large circle with their dive lights pointing upward to attract plankton. The plankton in turn attracts Manta Rays, which swoop in and do barrel rolls while directing the plankton into their open mouths. They often pass so close that divers have to duck to avoid contact. Anywhere from none to over two dozen mantas may attend the feast.

There are two isolated volcanic rock outcrops that also merit special mention... They are Molokini Crater, off Maui, and Lehua Rock, off Kauai. Both are hotspots for sightings of sharks, Giant Groupers, endangered Hawaiian Monk Seals – the second most endangered pinniped species in the world – and other pelagics. A Great White Shark with a length of 5m (16ft) was recently photographed at Molokini.

Chance, and Hawaii's location close to the middle of the Pacific Ocean, can lead to rare encounters with all sorts of passing non-residents, from Elephant Seals to Right Whales to Basking Sharks. More reliably, every year thousands of Humpback Whales make a regular migration from Alaska to Hawaii to breed. But be aware the law prohibits close approaches to them.

Occasionally, however, the animals swim by for a closer look at the divers, though most of us who visit Hawaii in winter will see whales cavorting at the surface in the distance but only hear them underwater. The whale songs are so loud that they often seem to be very close, and permeate the diver's body with a sensation that evokes all the mystery and suspense of the pelagic realm, reminding us of the likelihood of a large presence, just beyond the limits of vision.

GUADALUPE

Spectacular pelagics, spectacular scenery

Chris and Monique Fallows

On the Pacific side of the Baja Peninsula, about 340km (210 miles) from the port city of San Diego and roughly 24 hours away by dive boat, lies the volcanic island of Guadalupe.

The boat ride from San Diego can be rough as the storms that vent their anger on the waters of the Pacific often make their first landfall on the island's shores, so cruising through this turbulent water can test those who are not familiar with the ways of the sea. On many trips, however, the heaving waves beat a retreat and glassy seas and fair winds take their

place, and, since accurate weather forecasting is possible nowadays, predicting the best time to make the 24-hour crossing is a lot easier than in the past.

Huge cliffs, scarred by the many tracts that were once rivers of molten larva, rise steeply from the depths that surround this island and welcome you on arrival. It's a barren place, however... barely any vegetation is visible anywhere on the island and the only large terrestrial mammals you will see are the thousands of goats that now proliferate here. Human existence is concentrated around the island's southern end where Mexican fishermen make their headquarters in their annual pilgrimage to collect the highly valued Spiny Lobster. Around the northern end little human habitation is evident except for a few small derelict dwellings that now are home to the lobster fishermen who work this side of the island.

But, of course it's neither the lobster fishermen nor the goats and spectacular scenery that attract large dive vessels to the area from September to December. It is rather the greatest predatory fish modern man has ever known, the Great White Shark. Each autumn these magnificent hunters return to patrol these

Opposite A Great White Shark races into view in the clear blue waters of mystical Guadalupe.
Below The first glimpse of a Great White for those in the cage is an awe-inspiring moment, that being said, the surface viewing can be pretty good too.

waters in search of Yellowfin Tuna and three pinniped species that are found here. Unlike South Africa where the water at Great White Shark dive sites is seldom clear, the waters off Guadalupe can have visibility in the 25–30m (80–100ft) range and the water temperature is usually 17–21°C (63–70°F).

Most of the cage-diving activity takes place off the northeastern sector of the island in a sheltered bay that is surrounded by spectacular cliffs and valleys. Several cage-diving operations run out of San Diego, and three of them are present on a regular basis.

At the time of writing (first quarter of 2005), a new operation was being established to run out of Mexican waters (Guadalupe lies 232km (144 miles) from San Quentin) and hopefully the current situation, where the three existing operators seem to work well together in a relatively small area, will continue. Operators usually have to moor close to each other as

finding a good anchorage is a challenge... steep drop-offs and strong currents make prime mooring sites much sought-after.

All three of the regular operators have one or more cages attached to the their vessel's stern and one has a third cage which is sunk to around 6m (20ft). This offers a spectacular opportunity to see the sharks as they glide by above the cage; they are attracted to the boats by a constant supply of chum and bait in the form of tuna heads. Sharks come and go at will and at certain times several will be around one boat while other vessels may have only one – or none at all; as with all wildlife there is no guarantee of what will be encountered.

Divers are each allocated time in the cage on a rotational system to allow everyone a fair chance to see the sharks. As in most parts of the world (except in the Farallon Islands) the size of the sharks commonly seen varies between 3–4m (10–13ft) with exceptionally large or small

specimens being seen infrequently. As is the case with other sites, many sharks seen at Guadalupe return on an annual basis and a number of people who have visited the island frequently can point out known individuals or groups. This makes the encounter that much more special, knowing that you are diving with a regular favourite.

For the crews that work on the boats it is very rewarding as well, each year to see old sharky friends again, knowing they have survived the long-line fishermen and ruthless shark-finning fishermen who hunt them so indiscriminately elsewhere.

Obviously, each area around the world where Great White Sharks occur has its own peculiarities in terms of special behaviour that can be seen at that site and Guadalupe is no exception. Interesting behaviour that we noted was how much more dominant certain sharks were around the vessels.

In some cases a single large Great White, usually a female, would prevent other sharks from getting to the baits and would control the area around the boat as her own for hours on end. While a defined hierarchy is certainly a well-known trait of the Great Whites in South Africa, Australia and California, this was the first time we had witnessed this amount of dominance in Guadalupe.

Another interesting observation was the number of pilot fish we saw with the large females. It's something we see very little of in South Africa, and is usually only associated with animals of the open ocean, suggesting these sharks, particularly the big females who seemed to have the most pilot fish, cover great distances across open ocean to visit Guadalupe. Perhaps these big females are going somewhere far away to give birth, although it's generally believed this takes place off the Baja Peninsula.

On many days several sharks were seen, unfortunately bearing scars, suggesting contact with boats and rough handling both from cage-diving vessels and tuna fishermen in the area. A worrying threat to the area is the unprotected status that the Great White Shark has in Mexican waters. Only a week before our visit one of the cage-diving operators was engaged in a highly charged situation with a sport-fishing vessel that had actually come to hunt the sharks in the area. It is unlikely that the Guadalupe population is nearly as large as that off South Africa or other areas and as such is particularly vulnerable to this sort of unnecessary targeting.

The Great White Sharks of Guadalupe commonly poach hooked Yellowfin Tuna and other large fish from fishing vessels and, coupled with those that they hunt naturally, this is probably one of the reasons for them being there. Another is the assorted species of seals (pinnipeds) in the area including the highly endemic Guadalupe Fur Seals that were reduced to just a few individuals during the seal-hunting era. Each morning their wailing resonates through the cliffs and is unlike any other pinniped sound we have ever heard. It certainly adds to the uniqueness of the experience. These seals, as well as the California Sea Lions and young Northern Elephant Seals, are a prime source of a high-energy food for the Great White Shark.

As luck would have it, on our arrival to the island we witnessed a sub-adult Great White kill and consume what must have been either a young Guadalupe Fur Seal or young Sea Lion scarcely 300m (984ft) from the shore. For many of us who had visited the island for years this was the first known sighting of an actual predatory event.

Two days later we found clear evidence of another kill and the behaviour of the resident gulls indicates that they are very familiar with

Left *Male Northern Elephant Seals are massive and formidable predators, however even they occasionally fall prey to Great White Sharks.*

Opposite *Yellowfin Tuna are the main reason why long-range fishing boats visit Guadalupe and along with the seals form the main part of the Great White Shark's diet while the sharks are there.*

the hunting behaviour of the Great Whites at Guadalupe. The birds hover over kill sites knowing that a few scraps of the hapless seal are likely to come their way.

With more careful early morning observation no doubt more predatory events will be witnessed. Without going into too much detail a good way to do this is to simply get up just as the sun is rising and sit on the boat, scanning the first 500m (1640ft) of ocean from the shore. Look for large splashes, a jumping shark or one thrashing on the surface.

You can also watch the gulls in the area. See where they congregate above the water; see if a shiny surface slick is evident in the vicinity of the gulls and, if possible, make a closer inspection to determine whether any abnormal sort of scent is in the air, indicating a fresh kill.

If all three of these clues are present, even though the shark may not be, the chances are that you at the scene of a recent kill. But Great

Whites are not the only predators, and not every attack results in a kill: if you have the opportunity to go close to the Northern Elephant Seal rookeries that dot the shoreline be sure to look out for seals that have Cookie-cutter Shark bite scars. They take the form of circular plugs of skin that have been neatly removed from the flesh.

These sharks are found in the depths around the island, so the scars indicate that is where these seals also hunt.

While Great Whites are undoubtedly the reason for most to visit Guadalupe, be sure to look at the incredible rock formations (we even saw a massive landslide).

You can also enjoy the antics of the various seal and sea lion species found here and you may spot a couple of the less commonly seen pelagic birds that fly around the island. In addition to the big guys, and the Cookie-cutter, of course, Shortfin Mako, Blue and Oceanic

Whitetip Sharks have been reported around boats chumming for Great Whites – and quite obviously a this is a real bonus for anyone lucky enough to see them.

South Africa may have the most Great Whites Sharks that also display awesome natural hunting behaviour, but in my opinion, Guadalupe is the most spectacular locality in the world to see these animals (the Farallon Islands are not open to the public and no chumming is allowed there). Coupled with it great visibility Guadalupe is also on par or better than Australia as the best Great White Shark dive site around when these magnificent sharks are present.

The island truly is a very special place with some awesome animals and spectacular scenery. We can only hope the Mexican government will see fit to protect these lords of the ocean that for a brief period each year call the island their home.

SEA OF CORTEZ
Face to face with the Sea Lions of Los Islotes

Lawson Wood

Whizzing across the flat calm waters of the Sea of Cortez (Gulf of California), I could feel the skin of my face being pulled tight as we roared along at over 60 knots on *Rampage*, a 9m (30ft) bright yellow rigid inflatable boat (RIB). In 45 minutes this sleek and powerful machine with twin engines took the five of us 30km (19 miles) northwest of La Paz, past Isla Espiritu Santo, to a lonely guano-covered rock that is called Los Islotes (The Islets). I was glad I had plastered myself with factor 50 sun cream; other members of the party hadn't – and were rather raw and burnt at the end of the ride (or should I say flight!). Our mission was to record and photograph the underwater antics of one of the largest breeding colonies of California Sea Lions to be found in the waters of western Mexico.

The long finger of land that juts down from California off Mexico's west coast is known as Baja. It almost encloses a massive stretch of the Pacific named after the Spanish explorer Cortez. The sea has marine links with both the Pacific Ocean and a more ancient link with the Caribbean before the central American isthmus was formed.

Baja is probably better known for the almost total lack of development and the early heady days of Hotel California, surfing and tequila sunrises. Now, however, it has grown into a multicultural province with a number of new resort towns such as Cabo San Lucas, which sadly looks and feels like just another part of California. It's basically an American version of what they think Mexico should look like.

All this seems a far cry from splashing around, or should I rather say being splashed around by sea lions, but to get to these isolated pinnacles, there were three flight connections as well as a teeth-rattling speedboat journey. It felt as if time had stopped for a moment as the engines slowed to idle and we coasted to a standstill.

We could smell the guano from the seabird colonies instantly, but this was quickly forgotten as we looked onto a rookery of around 200 sea lions, snoozing, bickering and playfully diving into the water to haul themselves back out again and repeat the whole process. So that we would not frighten the animals off the rocks, we coasted quietly over the flat platform of smooth rock that separates the islets, rocking gently in our own wash.

But we definitely needn't have had any fear of disturbing them... no sooner had we approached the main rookery when the younger sea lions dived into the water and swam around us, barking – enticing us into the water.

Los Islotes is actually one huge, rocky spur that has been eroded in the centre, creating a flat rocky platform virtually at sea level, with boulders at either end. The rocky stacks are a designated nature park and no one is allowed to go ashore for fear of intrusion into the sea lions' lives. The rocks are covered in guano from nesting seagulls, Frigate Birds and the occasional pelican, and glistens in the afternoon sun. Topped by straggly cactuses, the easterly

Above *Playful and interested, sea lions readily approach snorkellers, as if mocking their ungainly movements.*

Opposite *Sea lions herd small schools of fish together before rushing in to feed on them.*

stack is more precipitous and is cut by a massive tunnel which is perfect for divers as the depth here is around 15m (45ft).

The larger bull sea lions each held court over their harem and would lunge threateningly towards us, bearing their teeth, but would leave us alone and allow us to interact with the juveniles as long as we kept clear of the resting sites of the females. Once we entered the water, we were quickly surrounded by inquisitive sea lions. Ungainly on land, their speed and agility in the water is quite daunting. The boisterous youngsters would flop their way over the smoothed-off boulders to their diving platforms and dive bomb us, pulling playfully at our fins, frightening the life out of me as they twisted and cavorted around the base of the rocks.

They would rush straight at your face, bare their teeth and whip away in a cloud of expelled air bubbles and perform a mind-boggling series of movements at breakneck speed. All of this left us with somewhat of a sense of inferiority regarding our own ungainly and clumsy performance in the water.

We found the best way to photograph the sea lions was to sneak up under the juveniles resting on the surface and compose the shot more as a silhouette. This captured the creature basking in the sun as it floated on its back on the surface supported by the air bladder next to its stomach. The shallows nearer the shore were also good and, by snorkelling, there was much less noise produced underwater and we were able to swim more freely with them as they herded fry into the shallows and then attacked the shoal from different angles.

In general terms the encounter far out-weighs any discomfort and travel time required to enjoy these playful pinnipeds and should be on the list of all divers and snorkellers.

From there, we cruised to a series of pinnacles called El Bajo. These pinnacles are covered on all sides by large Gorgonian Sea Fans and sponges, all of which appear to have

been pulled into curious flattened shapes, which we soon discovered were created by the almost constant tidal race that cuts through the rocky passes. On the bottom it runs in the opposite direction to that at the surface and there is a distinct halocline (a well-defined vertical salinity gradient in saline water) with the change in water temperature and salinity as the current is pushed into the Sea of Cortez from the Pacific. Exhilarating stuff amid

Opposite Juvenile sea lions are particularly nosy! They will come right up to you at great speed before turning away. What a delight!

Left Hammerhead sharks are commonly sighted on the offshore seamounts in the Sea of Cortez

Below Large numbers of sea lions are to be found at Los Islotes.

shoals of King Angelfish, barracuda, pufferfish, rabbitfish and exotic starfish. There were even some Longnose Hawkfish, which are more synonymous with the Red Sea.

Decompressing on the shotline we wondered whether we were fortunate or unfortunate at not encountering the large groups of hammerhead sharks – until a huge dark shadow passed overhead. While we had been searching for them around the pinnacles, they had been hovering quite close to the surface. It was only now, at the end of the dive, that we could appreciate the grace of these curiously shaped sharks and why they congregated in such vast numbers.

Once we were back on the boat, we drifted off station and as a bonus, and enjoyable end to the trip, caught sight of 10 or 12 giant mantas cruising serenely under the boat and feeding on the plankton in the tidal stream.

THE AUTHORS

Jack Jackson

Well known in the field of rugged exploration and the charting of unusual destinations in mountains, deserts and the sea, Jack Jackson is an advanced BS-AC diver who ran a sport diving operation and a diving boat in the Sudanese Red Sea for 12 years and has been diving exotic locations around the world ever since. Diving for over four decades, Jack is a Fellow of The Royal Photographic Society in Underwater Nature Photography and a Fellow of the Royal Geographical Society.

A professional photographer and author Jack writes and photographs regularly for a wide variety of books and magazines and has won two book awards and several photographic awards. See: http://www.jackjackson.co.uk

Lawson Wood

Lawson Wood was born in Duns, Scotland and has been scuba diving since 1965. Now with over 15 000 dives logged in all of the world's oceans, he is the author and co-author of a further 35 books. He is a founding member of the Marine Conservation Society, and founder of the first marine nature reserve in Scotland. He made photographic history in the UK by becoming the first person to gain Fellowships with the Royal Photographic Society and British Institute of Professional Photographers solely for underwater photography.

Lawson has won many awards for outstanding work in Marine Conservation. With his wife Lesley, he is based in the South of France, and Cayman Brac in the Cayman Islands, two of his favourite diving destinations.

Doug Perrine

Doug Perrine, a resident of Kailua-Kona, Hawaii, is widely regarded as one the world's foremost marine wildlife photographers. His award winning photographs have been published in hundreds of books, calendars, posters, postcards, and other graphic products, and thousands of magazines. He is also an accomplished author, with seven books and hundreds of magazine articles to his credit. His academic credentials include B.S. and M.A. Degrees in marine biology. He founded the stock photo library SeaPics.com, and operated for 18 years before selling it in 2003 to concentrate on his own writing and photography.

Chris and Monique Fallows

Chris and Monique Fallows specialize in shark conservation and wildlife photography. Their work has appeared in over 35 international natural history documentaries and on the covers of many of the world's most prestigious magazines. Their main aim is to portray the shark for what it is, a magnificent predator perfectly in control of its environment – and not a mindless killing machine as portrayed by the press. Chris and Monique spend up to 120 days per year at sea and over 50 days each year in the wild enjoying all nature has to offer.

Paul Lees

British photographer Paul Lees specializes in underwater photography. From his base in Phuket, southern Thailand, Paul has travelled throughout South and Southeast Asia, capturing vibrant images of the colourful, weird and often wonderful world of Asia's oceans.

Paul is a regular contributor to regional and international diving publications and has been responsible for two major publications; *Dive Guide Thailand* and *Andaman and Beyond* along with contributing to New Holland's *Top Dive Sites of the Indian Ocean* and *The Dive Atlas of the World*. More recently, Paul has been bringing the underwater world to the surface in the form of natural history documentaries and TV shows, including ABC Kane's, *The Living Edens* and the BBC's *Really Wild Show*.

Fiona McIntosh

Photo-journalist Fiona McIntosh has been fortunate to have dived all around the world since completing her first diving course in the dark, icy waters of Loch Long, in Scotland, 25 years ago. An adrenaline junkie, she loves diving with big pelagics, particularly sharks, and her encounters with Tiger Sharks in South Africa are her most exhilarating dives to date. Other highlights of researching her sections of this book were diving with Manta Rays at Guinjata Bay in Mozambique – which she rates as one of the top dive destinations in the world. Fiona has the enviable job of editing *Divestyle*, southern Africa's scuba diving magazine, and *Out There Adventure, Travel* and *Buyers' Guides*.

Rochelle Mutton

Rochelle Mutton developed a niche in diving and marine science reporting along the vast Western Australian coast, in 2000. Her career had begun on newspapers within the State in 1996, before overseas travel led to a four-month stint reporting in Zimbabwe in 1999.

After returning to Perth, WA, she traversed the State's 12,500km coastline and islands, working with leading marine photographers Peter and Margy Nicholas. Together they supplied news packages to Australian newspapers for three years. In September 2004, she relocated to Johannesburg, South Africa, where she is now based, and freelances foreign news for international broadcasters and newspapers.

Bob Halstead

Bob has been diving Papua New Guinea for 32 years – many say far too deep, for far too long – and was the first, with his diver wife Dinah, to set up a full-time sport diving business in the country in 1977. They coined the word 'muck' diving and still love PNG above all other areas, often returning from their new base in Cairns, Australia to lead exploratory and muck-diving expeditions. Last year they were the first to dive a P38 Lockheed Lightning fighter aircraft wreck recently discovered by villagers.

Bob says 'The adventure never ends!'

Steve Wong and Takako Uno

Stephen and Takako, a full-time husband-and-wife marine photojournalistic team since 1997, have had their work appear in marine and wildlife journals, and many exhibitions, such as *Wonders in Deep Waters by Stephen & Takako* (Hong Kong, 2003) and *Cetaceans* (Hong Kong, 2004). Their images have won numerous awards, including four successes in the prestigious BBC Wildlife Photographer of the Year competitions. In addition, Takako discovered a new species of nudibranch, now called *Takako's trapania*, and photographed a new species of Snapping Shrimp. Stephen has photographed a new species of octopus. The couple's images have also appeared in many books. See www.stephen-wong.com and www.takakouno.com

Rob Bryning

Born in 1960 into a naval family in Devon, England, Rob Bryning has always had a love of the sea and an abiding fascination with the underwater world.

His first diving experience took place when he was 16 years old and since then he has gone on to enjoy thousands of dives in the Maldives where he and his wife, Sam Harwood, own the live-aboards *MV Sea Queen* and *MV Sea Spirit*.

Rob and Sam have sailed the oceans and dived extensively throughout the world. Rob is an accomplished underwater photographer and videographer. Having lived in the Maldives for many years they now live in the UK with their two children.

ESSENTIAL INFORMATION

ARUBA, BONAIRE AND CURAÇAO (NETHERLANDS ANTILLES)

Climate: Sunny, except December–February; arid climate. Hottest August–October: lows of 24°C (75°F); highs rarely above 32°C (90°F). Average is 28°C (82°F) with a cooling breeze.

Best time to go and how to get there: The protected leeward coasts allow diving all year; more exposed sites are best dived in summer and autumn. Direct links to Amsterdam; North and Latin American links to Aruba and Curaçao, and further connections to Bonaire. Local airlines connect with Curaçao and Bonaire.

Water temperature: 24°C (75°F) in the cool season, but averages 27°C (80°F).

Visibility: Generally very clear, averaging 30m (100ft) or more on Bonaire and Curaçao. Aruba has good sandy beaches, so the sand can affect visibility on nearshore reefs.

Quality of corals and marine life: Corals are among the best in the Caribbean. Bonaire is the world leader in protecting underwater resources and Aruba and Curaçao are not far behind. All have good marine park systems. Observing coral spawning is a big event on all three islands during September–October. Marine life is diverse, prolific, tame and approachable.

Depth of dives: Often shallow – generally less than 40m (130ft) – but drop-offs and walls may descend deeper so act responsibly.

Recompression chambers:
BONAIRE
Saint Franciscus (Francisco) Hospital, Kaya Soeur Bartola, Kralendijk
Tel: +599 7178900.
and

CURAÇAO:
St Elisabeth Hospital
Tel: +599 9 4625100/4900
Chamber Tel: +599 9 4627457.

Snorkelling: All three islands are a paradise for snorkellers of all levels.

Dive practicalities: Except on their windy north and northeast coasts, and on deeper dives, diving in the ABCs is mostly relaxed and suitable for all levels of divers. Some dives have moderate currents where intermediate skills are preferable. Operators offer extensive facilities, diving courses and equipment for hire (larger ones offer Nitrox and technical diving).

Operators can organize vehicles for shore diving. Double-cab pick-ups are preferred, but you have to ask for them, take essential gear only and don't leave items in an unattended vehicle. Some shore dives on Curaçao are accessed from private property so there may be a small charge. Recently on Bonaire, thieves have been cutting fuel pipes to steal fuel.

AZORES

Climate: 17–24°C (63–75°F). Temperate, cloudy with year-round rains. Storms and higher humidity in winter (October–April).

Best time to go and how to get there: Ocean Sunfish are found year round, but mainly from June–September. The Azores are well served by carriers from Lisbon.

Water temperatures: 14–24°C (57–75°F).

Visibility: Winter, 5–15m (16–50ft), but 50m (165ft) on a good summer's day.

Quality of marine life: Good. Sunfish, whales and dolphins, Manta Rays, sharks, barracuda, octopuses and turtles.

Depth of dives: Scuba diving at most dive sites is less than 25m (80ft).

Recompression (hyperbaric) chambers:
SÃO MIGUEL:
Clube Naval De Ponta Delgada
9500 Ponta Delgada
São Miguel
Tel: +351 296 23005;
Fax: +351 296 26383
and
FAIAL:
Hospital Da Horta
9900 Horta
Tel: +35129 2200200;
Fax: +35129 2293144

Snorkelling: Snorkelling is probably the only way to have long encounters with sunfish.

Dive practicalities: Operators offer scuba diving and gear for hire. Wearing an exposure suit is advisable to protect against jellyfish.

Whale watching is topside only (except on dolphin swimming programmes, and for scientists with permits).

BAHAMAS

Climate: 24–32°C (75–90°F). Generally good except in the hurricane season, July–November.

Best time to go and how to get there: May–September, but all year is possible. The area is well served with flights to other areas.

Water temperature: 24–28°C (75–82°F) all year, but a full 3-5mm wet suit is required.

Visibility: 30m (100ft) or more.

Quality of corals and marine life: Very good; Elkhorn corals in the shallows are superb. Marine life excellent, huge diversity.

Depth of dives: 12–33m (40–110ft).

Recompression (hyperbaric) chambers:
NASSAU:
Tel: +1242 362 4025

Grand Bahama Island
Tel: +1242 373 1244.

Snorkelling: Superb in all regions.

Dive practicalities: Beginner–advanced.

BALI

Climate: Tropical; rains November–March, dry April–October. August–September temperatures 23–29°C (73–84°F).

Best time to go and how to get there: Sunfish are found year round but the best time is August to the end of September. Bali is a major Indonesian international gateway; direct links to many other countries.

Water temperature: Varies by site, from 28°C (82°F) in minimal current areas such as Tulamben, to possibly below 15°C (60°F) in areas prone to strong currents, such as Nusa Lembongan and Nusa Penida. Even at Crystal Bay the drop can be marked, from 25°C (77°F) at the surface, to below 18°C (65°F) at depth.

Visibility: At Nusa Lembongan and Nusa Penida usually 15–30m (50–100ft). The deeper part of Tulamben that is occasionally visited by sunfish can have 50m (165ft) visibility.

Quality of corals and marine life: Lush soft and stony corals in Nusa Penida. Besides Ocean Sunfish, Manta Rays, Eagle Rays, thresher and other species of sharks, Bali also has an incredible diversity of weird creatures, such as Mimic Octopuses, Pygmy Sea Horses, sea moths, and Flamboyant Cuttlefish.

Depth of dives: Sunfish can be found at all depths, but usually below 30m (100ft); take note the dive practicalities below.

Decompression (hyperbaric) chamber: SANGLAH GENERAL HOSPITAL: USUP Sanglah Denpasar JI. Diponegoro, Denpasar 80114 Bali, Tel: +62 361 227911; Fax: +62 361 22426 www.sanglahbalihospital.com email info@sanglahbalihospital.com

Snorkelling: Can be done off beaches in most areas but beware of strong currents, stonefish and urchins.

Dive practicalities: Sunfish are most often sighted at Nusa Lembongan's Blue Corner, Crystal Bay next to Nusa Penida, Tepekong off Padangbai and off the Drop-Off in Tulamben.

With the exception of Tulamben, all of the above dive sites can have strong currents. Be aware that Tepekong, Blue Corner and Crystal Bay can have downwelling currents.

In strong currents many diving computers lock up in error mode. So, pay close attention to depths.

By boat from resorts on Bali, it takes between 30 and 90 minutes to reach these sites.

CAPE COAST, SOUTH AFRICA

Climate: Usually mild 17–21°C (63–70°F)

Best time to go and how to get there: Best May–September. International links between Cape Town and all other parts of the world.

Water temperatures: 15–17°C (60–63°F) but off Dyer Island the water can reach 20°C (68°F) under abnormal conditions.

Visibility: From 2–15m (6–50ft).

Quality of marine life: Very good.

Recompression (hyperbaric) chamber: CAPE TOWN: Kingsbury Hospital Wilderness Road Claremont Tel: +27 21 6704000.

Snorkelling: Only sensible in cages.

Dive practicalities: For free-floating cages an entry level scuba qualification is required; no qualifications required for fixed cages.

As all scuba diving is within 1m (40in) of the surface, there are no decompression issues.

All boats have trauma kits and crew certified in first aid.

CENTRAL CARIBBEAN: TOBAGO, ARUBA, BELIZE, HONDURAS, MEXICO, CAYMAN ISLANDS

Climate: 26–35°C (79–95°F). Generally good, except in hurricane season (June–November). North Sound, Cayman Islands slightly cooler.

Best time to go and how to get there: Best time for Whale Sharks and Manta Rays in these areas is May–September.

In the Caymans May–September is the best time to see Green Turtles and Hawksbill Turtles, but it is possible all year.

Regular flights link all areas to the USA and elsewhere.

Water temperature: All areas 24–29°C (75–84°F).

Visibility: All areas 25–50m (80–150ft), but 10–25m (33–80ft) at North Sound, Caymans.

Quality of corals and marine life: Both very good in all areas.

Depth of dives: 12–33m (40–110ft); but 18–30m (60–100ft) at North Sound, Caymans.

Recompression (hyperbaric) chambers: BELIZE: Lions Clinic Chamber San Pedro Ambergris Caye Tel: +501 226 3195. *and* GEORGETOWN: Cayman Hyperbaric Services Tel: +1 345 949 2989 Georgetown Hospital Tel: +1 345 949 8600.

Snorkelling: Very good in all areas, and off-shore locations in the Caymans.

Dive practicalities: Beginner–advanced. Full 3–5mm wet suit is necessary in all areas.

In the Caymans a wet suit will also give protection against stingrays as some of them can be aggressive.

CUBA

Climate: Semitropical, with two seasons. December–March, up to 26ºC (80ºF); July–August, up to 32ºC (90ºF). Humidity and rains highest September–October. Hurricanes rare but possible August–November.

Best time to go and getting there: Diving all year round, though winter seas are slightly rougher. The Pirate Coast on the Isla de la Juventud is protected and can be dived even in heavy rain. February–May are among the best months. The wet season is May–October. Direct flights link Havana to Europe, Canada, Mexico and nearby South American gateways. Restricted flights operate from Miami. Charter flights are available direct to larger resort areas from Europe. Air link between Havana and Isla de la Juventud; then 40km (25 miles) by road to the El Colony Hotel Diving Complex.

Water temperature: Averages 28ºC (82ºF) in summer and 24ºC (75ºF) in winter.

Visibility: Averages 30m (100ft) plus.

Quality of corals and marine life: By Caribbean standards the corals are extremely good; marine life is one of the best – diverse, prolific, very tame and approachable.

Depth of dives: Generally less than 30m (100ft), but some sites require short decompression stops. Others descend deeper than sports divers should dive, so act responsibly.

Recompression chambers:
HAVANA:
La Habana Hyperbaric Medical Centre,
Hospital Naval 'Dr Luis Diaz Soto',
Havana del Este
Tel: +53 7 973266
and
GERONA:
Hospital General Docente Heroes del Baire,
Avenue 39 Nueva Gerona
Tel: +53 61 23012
and
CÁRDENAS:
Hospital 'Julio Arietegui', Centro de Medicina Subacuatica,
Carretera de Cardenas, Km 2,
Cárdenas, Matanzas
Tel: +53 45 22114
and
CIENFUEGOS:
Hospital Clínico Quirúrgico Universitario,
Cienfuegos
Tel: +53 432 513911
and
SANTIAGO DE CUBA:
Hospital Militar 'Castillo Duany', Punta Blanca,
Santiago de Cuba
Tel: +53 22 26471
and
ISLA DE LA JUVENTUD:
Hotel El Colony, Carretera de la Siguanea, Km 41,
Colony Isla de la Juventud
Tel: +53 46 398240
and
ULISES RESEARCH VESSEL:
Barco de Investigaciones Ulises, Ciudad de La Habana
Tel: +53 7 8617643.

Snorkelling: A paradise for snorkellers of all levels, but best at sites reached only by boat.

Dive practicalities: Diving is mostly relaxed and apart from the deeper dives, suitable for all levels of divers. Operators offer diving courses, extensive facilities and equipment for hire.

FRENCH POLYNESIA: RANGIROA, RURUTU

Climate: 21–28ºC (70–82ºF). Generally good all year, but periodic storms in winter.

Best time to go and how to get there: Humpback Whales, October–November; all year for sharks, mantas and dolphins. Airlines link the islands to France, US and NZ.

Water temperature: 18–24ºC (65–75ºF).

Visibility: 25–60m (82–197ft).

Quality of corals and marine life: Corals good in Tahiti and northern atolls but less so in Rurutu due to cooler waters. Marine life excellent. Wide diversity of Indo-Pacific species including many exotic nudibranchs and other invertebrates as well as big pelagics.

Depth of dives: Over 35m (115ft) in the Tiputa Pass and on all reef dives. Humpback Whale encounters by snorkel only.

Decompression (hyperbaric) chambers:
TAHITI:
Jean Prince Army Medical Centre
Tel: +689 462299 or 463153
and
Mama'o Hospital:
Tel: +689 466262
No direct line: ask for the 'caisson hyperbar'.

Snorkelling: Superb on the shallow reefs as the drop-offs tend to start in shallow water.

Dive practicalities: Beginner–advanced, but deep dive experience is recommended. Tahiti is also perfect for learning to dive. A full 3–5mm wet suit is required to dive the southern islands.

FIJI

Climate: Tropical, 20–30ºC (68–86ºF). Some variation between different islands, and the islands' wet east and dry west sides. Generally November–April is warmer and wetter; May–October is cooler, windier.

Best time to go and how to get there: All year, unless to see Bull Sharks; they are absent from Shark Reef late October–December; best diving season varies by location. Fiji linked by air with Europe, North America, Australia, New Zealand and various South Pacific islands.

Water temperatures: September–October 24ºC (75ºF); 30ºC (86ºF) February–March.

Visibility: 12–40m (40–130ft).

Quality of corals and marine life: Famed for the beauty and abundance of its soft corals. Stony corals vary by location. The 1998 El Niño event hit many reefs hard; others are in near pristine condition. Excellent marine life with a good mix of large and small species.

Recompression (hyperbaric) chambers:
SUVA:
Suva Private Hospital
120 Amy Street,
Suva, Viti Levu Island
Tel: +679 331 3355
recompression@connect.com.fj
and
SAVUSAVU:
Fiji Recompression Chamber Facility
Main Street, Savusavu, Fiji Island
Tel: +679 885 0630
Mobile: +679 999 3506
Email: recompression@connect.com.fj

Snorkelling: Excellent in most locations, but not recommended for the Big Fish Encounter.

Dive practicalities: Open Water certification required.

GUADALUPE

Climate: Mild, daytimes 20–22°C (68–72°F).

Best time to go and how to get there:
Late September–late November from San Diego. Boats depart from various San Diego marinas for the 24-hour crossing to Guadalupe.

Water temperatures: 17–21°C (63–70°F).

Visibility: Often exceeds 30m (100ft), seldom under 15m (50ft).

Quality of marine life: Corals not relevant, but marine life is good for large species, including seal species, Yellowtail Tuna, and, during the summer months, game fish and Horn Sharks closer to shore.

Depth of dives: Most cage-dives are off the stern of the various dive boats; some operators sink extra cages to around 13m (43ft).

Recompression (hyperbaric) chambers:
Call the DAN Emergency Hotline 919 684 8111 (or 919 684 4326 collect) for assistance.

SAN DIEGO:
Emergency airlifts are possible from the island of Guadalupe to San Diego. Operators have VHF and SSB radios and are in contact with mainland USA should an emergency evacuation be necessary. The US Navy has a hyperbaric facility in San Diego harbour.

Snorkelling: All cage-diving is done purely with scuba or by using a hookah system.

Dive practicalities: Mexican government permission is required to land on the island; and a permit, obtained before departure for Guadalupe, is required to fish in its vicinity. Further details are available from operators.

HAWAII

Climate: Tropical to sub-tropical, varies by location. Wetter on the eastern sides of the islands. On coasts usually 20–30°C (68–86°F).

Best time to go and how to get there:
Year round, except for Humpback Whales (present December–April). Generally calmer seas April–September. Hawaii is a major destination; many airlines and local carriers serve it.

Water temperatures: 22–28°C (72–82°F), warmest June–October.

Visibility: 10–50m (33–165ft), typically 30–40m (100–130ft) offshore; inshore visibility can be reduced by the surge accompanying ocean swells, that are usually largest in winter.

Quality of corals and marine life: Coral health is generally good, but Crown-of-Thorns Starfish are present, and some bleaching and coral disease have been noted. Low diversity and limited reef development, particularly on the youngest island, Hawaii. Marine life's low diversity and high endemism make Hawaii a good place for unique small reef creatures not seen elsewhere. Offshore, Hawaii shares its pelagic life with other tropical locations and is considered an excellent area for pelagic encounters.

Depth of dives: Generally 30m (100ft) or

less, although the bottom drops off quickly to depths of thousands of metres in some areas.

Recompression (hyperbaric) chamber:
HONOLULU:
Kuakini Hospital:
347 North Kuakini Street
Tel: +1 808 587 3425.

Snorkelling: Offshore activities are on snorkel, but you must be at ease in open water.

Dive practicalities: A basic certification for manta night dives and an advanced for Lehua Rock or backside Molokini.

KWAZULU-NATAL, SOUTH AFRICA

Climate: Summer rainfall, more tropical to the north. Winters 10–25°C (50–77°F); summers 20–38°C (68–100°F).

Best time to go and how to get there:
Spotted Raggedtooth Sharks: Quarter Mile Reef, Sodwana Bay, December–March, Aliwal Shoal, July–December; Tiger Sharks: Aliwal Shoal, January–June; Bull (Zambezi) Sharks: Protea Banks, October–May. International and local links to Durban, good roads in region.

Water temperatures: Sodwana Bay:19–29°C (66–84°F); Aliwal Shoal/Protea Banks: 19–28°C (66–82°F).

Visibility: Sodwana Bay: 14–21m (45–69ft) but can be 35m (115ft) plus. Aliwal Shoal/Protea Banks: 5–30m (16–100ft).

Quality of corals and marine life: Excellent and abundant.

Depth of dives: 10–30m (33–100ft).

Recompression (hyperbaric) chambers:
DURBAN:
St Augustine's Hospital
107 Chelmsford Road, Berea Mayville
Tel: +27 31 2685000
Chamber: Tel: +27 31 2685255
and

Natal Hyperbaric Centre
Tel: +27 31 3053069
NOTE: Not all chambers are permanently manned, in the event of any problems, contact DAN: 0800 020111 or +27 11 254 1112.

Snorkelling: Possible on Quarter Mile Reef.

Dive practicalities: Sodwana Bay and protected sites on Aliwal Shoal: Open Water or equivalent. Protea Banks and deeper, more exposed sites at Aliwal Shoal: Advanced.

MALAYSIA

Climate: 26–30°C (80–86°F), tropical, warm and humid all year and rarely below 20°C (68°F) except on high ground. Monsoon winds influence the climate but strong winds are rare. Typhoons miss this region by several hundred kilometres, thus Borneo is called 'the land below the wind'. Only in the north of Peninsular Malaysia's east coast and on Layang-Layang does tourism need to close during the monsoon seasons. Hence Pulau Perhentian, Pulau Redang and Layang-Layang are closed November–March.

Best time to go and how to get there:
Each area has two main seasons, one drier and the other the monsoon season.

In Peninsular Malaysia, the west is drier November–March, and wetter April–October. The east coast is wetter November–March and drier April–October. Sabah's west coast is wettest June–December, and driest January–May. Layang-Layang can have bad weather at any time but its best weather is April–September. The islands around Pulau Sipadan and Pulau Sangalaki can be dived year round but the weather is best May–October.

August is the high season for both local holidays and turtle nesting.

To reach Peninsular Malaysia fly to Kuala Lumpur, then take a domestic flight to Pulau Tioman or Pulau Redang or the nearest town for onward land and ferry travel to other islands. To visit East Malaysia fly to Kota Kinabalu, then special flights go to Layang-Layang or domestic flights connect to Tawau for Pulau Sipadan and other islands off

Semporna. From Tawau go by helicopter to Pulau Sipadan or by road to Semporna and then a speedboat to the islands. For Lankayan take a domestic flight to Sandakan then carry on by speedboat. Labuan can be reached by ferry from Kota Kinabalu as well as by air.

Water temperatures: 25°C (77°F) over deep water in the cooler season, 31°C (88°F) in warm season; 30°C (86°F) in shallow water.

Visibility: Approaches 60m (200ft) in good conditions at Layang-Layang and Sipadan and is rarely below 30m (100ft). At Pulau Perhentian, Pulau Lang Tengah and Pulau Tioman it is between 3–30m (10–100ft). At Pulau Aur, Pulau Redang and Pulau Tenggol, over 30m (100ft) is common, and 15–30m (45–100ft) around Pulau Lankayan. Pulau Mabul and Pulau Kapalai are muck-diving destinations: visibility 3–15m (10–45ft).

Quality of corals and marine life: Corals very good. Marine life diverse and prolific, and often very tame and inquisitive. Large pelagics may be encountered even inshore.

Depth of dives: The reefs at Layang-Layang and Pulau Sipadan descend to depths greater than sport divers should dive; act responsibly.

Recompression (hyperbaric) chambers:
PERAK:
Peninsular Malaysia (at Lumut Naval Base):
32100 Lumut, Perak
Tel: +605 6837090 Fax: +605 6837169
Website: www.hatl.gov.my/divemed.htm
and
Centre for Wound Care and Hyperbaric Medicine (Hyperbaric Health)
16, Persiaran Greentown 1,
Greentown Business Centre,
30450 Ipoh, Perak
Tel: +605 2426237
or
+605 C-H-A-M-B-E-R
Website: www.hbomalaysia.com
and
KUANTAN:
Kuantan Naval Base
Tg. Gelang

25990 Kuantan,
Pahang
Tel: +609 513 3333
and
LABUAN:
East Malaysia (at Labuan)
Pejabat Selam, Markas Wilayah Laut Dua
87007 Labuan
Tel: +608 741 2122
and
SINGAPORE:
Naval Medicine & Hyperbaric Centre
24-hr Emergency Hotline: (+65) 6758 1733
and
Tan Tock Seng Hospital Hyperbaric Medicine Centre
11 Jalan Tan Tock Seng
Basement 1 Tan Tock Seng Hospital
308433 Singapore
Tel: +65 6355 9021/22
Email: hbot1@singnet.com.sg
and
PALAU MABU:
Borneo Divers has a two-person chamber in Palau Mabu: Information@BorneoDivers.info

Snorkelling: Good from the shore or in shallow water over coral reefs for all levels.

Dive practicalities: Apart from Layang-Layang and Sipadan's Turtle Cavern, Malaysian diving is relaxed and suitable for all standards of divers. Layang-Layang can have strong currents and heavy swells, so carry a high-visibility late-deployment SMB, rescue tube or flag. Operators offer diving courses and gear for hire. Live-aboard boats cover most diving areas off Semporna, from Semporna.

MALDIVES

Climate: 24–30°C (75–86°F). A complex weather pattern: a drier northeast monsoon season and wetter southwest monsoon season.

Best time to go and how to get there: All year, March–April has good visibility. Charter flights to Hulule airport on Malé and regular links to South Africa, Europe and the Far East.

Water temperature: 24–30°C (75–86°F).

Visibility: Average of 20–25m (65–80ft).

Quality of corals and marine life: Both are good, with over 1000 marine species.

Depth of dives: Banned beyond 30m (100ft).

Recompression (hyperbaric) chambers:
NORTH MALÉ:
Bandos Medical Clinic and Hyperbaric Centre:
Bandos Island Resort, Republic of Maldives
Tel: +960 44 0088, Fax +960 44 0060
Email: maldives@daneurope.org
and
KURUMATHI (RASDHOO):
Kuramathi Medical Centre:
Kuramathi Island Resort
Emergency. Tel: +960 77 3485
Email: ktimdctr@kuramathi.com.mv
and
KANDOLUDHOO:
Kandoludhoo Divers Rescue:
Kandoludhoo Island Resort
Tel: +960 77 3485

Snorkelling: Superb.

Dive practicalities: Qualified divers have to produce proof of certification.

MILNE BAY, PAPUA NEW-GUINEA

Climate: 25–30°C (77–86°F) Tropical, rains highly variable, no well-defined wet season. South East trades May–November. Cyclones are possible but they are very rare.

Best time to go and how to get there: Mantas all year, best May–November; Whale Sharks occasionally October–January; hammerhead sharks all year, best June–December. Good air links to Australia, Japan, Philippines and other destinations.

Water temperatures: At manta sites the water is usually 25°C (77°F) (July–August), 29°C (84°F) (December–January).
The water is generally a degree or so cooler than further north in Milne Bay Province.

Visibility: 30m (99ft) or more, averaging 10–15m (33–45ft) at Manta Ray sites.

Quality of corals and marine life: Corals mostly excellent; and reefs are famed for their diversity and richness of marine life.

Depth of dives: Best to 20m (66ft). Reefs typically shallow topped, 5–8m (16–25ft) but can slope steeply to 40m (130ft) or more.

Recompression (hyperbaric) chamber:
PORT MORESBY:
Melanesian Hyperbaric Services Ltd
Port Moresby Airport
Tel: +675 325 9599 (chamber).
An aircraft for emergency evacuations is available from Airlines PNG.

Snorkelling: Usually excellent in sheltered, calm waters but other reefs may be subject to tidal currents. Check with your dive master.

Dive practicalities: Take personal dive equipment except for tank and weights. Safety sausages and torches (flashlights) are essential.

MOZAMBIQUE

Climate: Average 27–31°C (80–88°F), low 16°C (61°F) and high 40°C (105°F) possible. Dry April–September, rainy October–March.

Best time to go and how to get there: All year round for Manta Rays, and December–March for Whale Sharks. Regular air links between main centres, while feeder airlines serve smaller centres. Roads are reasonable.

Water temperature: 25–29°c (77–84°f).

Visibility: 5–20m (16–66ft).

Quality of corals and marine life: Good corals, great variety of marine life.

Depth of dives: 10–30m (33–100ft).

Recompression (hyperbaric) chamber:
RICHARDS BAY (South Africa):
The Bay Hospital

Kruger Rand Road
Sunward Park
Richards Bay
KwaZulu-Natal
Tel: +27 357806111; Fax: +27 227191037

Snorkelling: Good in protected bays.

Dive practicalities: Advanced qualification required.

PHILIPPINES

Climate: 23–36°C (73–97°F), tropical, with pronounced seasons: dry November–February, wet June–October, when typhoons can occur in the northern part of the country.

Best time to go and how to get there: All year for most areas, but not the far north. It's reliably calm everywhere April–May, with peak season December–June. The Tubbataha reefs are comfortably dived March–June only. Fly to Manila or Cebu, then domestic flights link to all major destinations including Puerto Princesa where live-aboard boats link to the Tubbataha Reefs. Good ferry services to many islands, easing the cost of diver's weight and decompression issues when flying.

Water temperatures: 25–31°C (77–88°F) depending on season.

Visibility: It is usually excellent, over 40m (130ft) on a flood tide.

Quality of corals and marine life: Over 7000 islands mean many reefs. Where not damaged by destructive fishing and over-exploitation, great biodiversity and large and colourful gorgonias. Many damaged reefs are being allowed to regenerate. Diverse, prolific marine life; large pelagics regularly encountered on offshore reefs.

Depth of dives: Many open water reefs descend to great depths, so dive responsibly.

Recompression (hyperbaric) chambers:
SUBIC BAY:
Subic Bay Freeport Zone

SBMA

Olongapo City

Tel: +63 47 2527952

and

MANILA:

AFP Medical Centre

V. Lunar Rd

Quezon City

Tel: +63 2 9207183/4262701

and

CAVITE CITY:

Sangley Recompression Chamber

NSWG, Philippine Fleet,

Naval Base Cavite,

Sangley Point,

Cavite City,

Tel: +63 46 5242061

and

BATANGAS CITY:

St Patricks Hospital,

Lopez Jaena St,

Batangas City 4200

Tel: +63 43 7238388 or 7232167

or 7237089 (chamber)

and

CEBU CITY:

VISCOM Station Hospital

Camp Lapu Lapu

Lahug

Tel: +63 32 233 9942

Evacuation Assistance:

AFP Search & Rescue Facilities

GHQ, Philippine Air Force

Villamor Air Base, Pasay City

Metro Manila

Tel: +63 2 9117996 or 2 9116385

Snorkelling: Good from the shore and in shallow water over coral reefs.

Dive practicalities: Strong currents possible in any open water area, especially during spring tides. On the Tubbataha Reefs experienced divers should accompany novices. Carry a high-visibility delayed deployment surface marker buoy or flag, a power whistle and an old CD-ROM for use as a heliograph.

Land-based operators offer diving courses in several languages, and have gear for hire. Live-aboard boats don't normally offer courses and only have a small selection of gear for hire.

RED SEA: ISRAEL, JORDAN, NORTHERN EGYPT, SOUTHERN EGYPT AND SUDAN

Climate: *Israel, Jordan, northern Egypt:* Warm, mostly dry winters, average 20°C (68°F), but cold and windy out to sea, so a dry suit, semi-dry suit or thick wet suit is recommended. Hot, dry summers, average 35°C (95°F), but the winds at sea can be strong. Wet suits are fine but also have warm clothes available if on a boat. You are only exposed to the heat when travelling on land.

Southern Egypt:

Summers hot and humid on land but winds at sea can be strong. Thin wet suits are fine but have warm clothes. You are exposed to the heat only while travelling on land. Winters are pleasantly warm on land but cold out to sea, so have warm clothing on boats. In summer the winds keep Brothers Islands, Elphinstone Reef, Dædalus Reef, Gezîret Zabargad, Rocky Islet and St John's at a pleasant temperature when the water is warm enough for a thin wet suit.

Sudan:

Winters warm and dry but offshore winds can be very strong so have warm clothes on the boat. Summers can reach 47°C (117°F) on land. On a live-aboard, you are only exposed to the heat when travelling on land. At sea the temperature is comfortable but humid. Thin wet suits are best in winter and Lycra Skins fine in summer.

Best time to go and how to get there:

Israel, Jordan, northern Egypt and southern Egypt: The whole region is dived all year round but is best in summer, May–September. High season for bookings is winter, October–April. Brothers Islands, Dædalus Reef, Gezîret Zabargad, Rocky Islet and St John's are best dived May–July. Charters are run during August–September but the sea can be rough. Elphinstone is best dived April–September.

Sudan:

Dived all year, but most live-aboard boats operating out of Port Sudan do so only in winter, though it can get very windy and rough at that time. Best times are May–July and September. Avoid August as heavy rains in nearby Ethiopia

cause generally poor weather and south winds called Haboobs, which bring dust and sand.

In Israel, Eilat airport handles small aircraft only; some divers fly to Tel Aviv, then by road to Eilat. Charter flights use the military airport at Ovda, 40 minutes by road from Eilat.

For Jordan most divers go to Aqaba after flying into Amman, but the Eilat/Aqaba border is now open so flying via Israel can be cheaper.

Egypt's Râs el Naqb airport serves Taba and Nuweiba in the Sinai; entry to Israel is via Taba, but Egyptian custom officers can be a problem here. In addition to Râs el Naqb, there are Egyptian international airports at Râs Nusrâni (Sharm el Sheikh Airport) for the Sinai, south of Hurghada for Hurghada and El Gouna and north of Marsa 'Alam for the deep south. There is also a small airport at El Gouna. All except El Gouna have direct charter flights or connecting flights via Cairo.

Live-aboard boats for the offshore marine park islands and reefs use Hurghada or Port Ghalib International Marina at Marsa 'Alam.

For Sudan, air connections have improved but it is better to go via Cairo to Port Sudan than direct to Khartoum because connecting flights between Khartoum and Port Sudan are subject to delays.

Most reliable are the flights from Jeddah in Saudi Arabia but these are only available to Saudi Arabian nationals or expatriates working there. Taking a live-aboard boat from Egypt is a good option.

NOTE: If your passport indicates you've visited Israel, or intend doing so, you will be refused entry to Saudi Arabia.

Water temperatures: *Israel, Jordan and northern Egypt:* summer average 25°C (77°F), 19°C (66°F) in winter.

Southern Egypt, south to Sudan border: summer average is 28°C (82°F) offshore and 30°C (86°F) on fringing reefs, but as low as 23°C (73°F) in winter. Brothers Islands, Elphinstone Reef, Dædalus Reef, Gezîret Zabargad, Rocky Islet and St John's average 27°C (81°F) in summer.

Sudan: averages 28°C (82°F) in summer, 27°C (81°F) in winter. There can be highs of 30°C (86°F) in places; surface patches beside reefs can be hot.

Visibility: At least 20m (65ft) on fringing or nearshore reefs except near ports and where divers or currents stir up the silt, 30–40m (100–130ft) is common over deep water.

Quality of corals and marine life: Corals are among the best of their species anywhere with a high density of stony and soft corals and gorgonias. Some diver and construction damage near major coastal towns or ports but generally stony corals get better further south towards central Sudan and are best on offshore reefs. Marine life is very good, with invertebrates, and reef and pelagic fish. Many shark species on the offshore reefs. The Red Sea's greatest density and diversity of pelagic species, especially sharks, is off Sudan – thanks to the absence of large-scale commercial fishing.

Depth of dives: From the surface to depths well beyond the accepted limits of sport or recreational technical diving. Depths of 30–40m (100–130ft) are common for experienced divers but 25m (80ft) is deep enough to see most things of interest.

Recompression (hyperbaric) chambers:
Israel:
Yoseftal Hospital, Eilat
Tel. (chamber): +972 0 8 6358023
Jordan:
The Princess Haya (Bint El-Hussein) Hospital
Aqaba.
Tel. +962 0 3 2014111
Northern and southern Egypt:
Sharm el Sheikh opposite the naval harbour:
Hyperbaric Medical Centre
Tel: +20 62660922/3; Fax: +20 62661011
E-mail: hyper_med_center@sinainet.com.eg
and
El Gouna Hospital north of Hurghada
Tel: +20 12 187550 or +20 65 549709 or +20 (69) 660 922-3
24-hr emergency number +20 (12) 212 42 92
and
North of Marsa 'Alam in Ecolodge Shagra Village at Marsa Shagra.
Tel: +20 195 100262.
Sudan:
The working hyperbaric chambers in Jeddah (Saudi Arabia) are not available to most divers.

The nearest chambers available without bureaucratic problems are at Marsa Shagra and El Gouna (Egypt) so dive conservatively.

Snorkelling: Almost everywhere, except where sharks are common, as they may mistake a snorkeller on the surface for a fish in trouble.

Dive practicalities: Ensure good buoyancy control to avoid damaging the coral and wear protective clothing against sunburn, fire coral and stinging hydroids; at night beware of Lionfish. Ear infections, often fungal, are common in divers and snorkellers in the Red Sea. Apply an ear-drying agent after each dive.

Operators in the north often have extensive facilities, offer diving courses, are well stocked and have gear for hire. Larger ones also offer Nitrox and technical diving. Those in the south have minimal equipment so you are generally better off if self-sufficient. Take along all equipment, spares, prescription medicines, decongestants, batteries and film. Sudan's operators don't stock gear and there are no dive shops. Good batteries, even toilet paper, can be unobtainable.

SANGALAKI

Climate: 26–30°C (80–86°F), tropical, humid. Rarely below 20°C (68°F).

Best time to go and how to get there:
The islands around Pulau Sangalaki can be dived year round. If going through Malaysia fly to Kota Kinabalu in Malaysian Borneo, then to Tawau. From Tawau fly to Tarakan in Indonesian Kalimantan, and from there 145km (90 miles) by boat directly to the dive resort. Or go by ferry from Tawau to Tarakan. It is large, comfortable and runs six days a week, but not on Indonesian public holidays. There's no weight limit for baggage so you can take a lot of equipment without excess baggage charges. The trip takes three hours.

If travelling through Indonesia, there are two possibilities: from Singapore direct to Balikpapan and then to Berau (Tanjung Redeb), where a boat will take you down the River Berau and across the sea to the resort. Alternatively, fly to Jakarta on Java or

Denpasar in Bali (both in Indonesia), then to Balikpapan on Kalimantan and then via Samarinda to Tanjung Redeb (Berau). From there you take a boat as above.

Water temperatures: 25°C (77°F) over deep water in the cooler season; up to 31°C (88°F) in the warmer season.

Visibility: Varies: 15–30m (50–100ft) plus.

Quality of corals and marine life: Corals very good except at Derawan; generally, reefs furthest offshore are in the best condition. Marine life diverse and prolific, often very tame and inquisitive. Large pelagics may be encountered, even inshore.

Depth of dives: Generally not deep.

Recompression (hyperbaric) chambers:
SABAH:
Sangalaki Dive Lodge
PO Box 16360
88000 Kota Kinabalu
Sabah, Malaysia
Tel: +60 88 242336 (Kota Kinabalu)
Mobile: +60 16 8181976

Snorkelling: Good from the shore and in shallow water over coral reefs for all levels.

Dive practicalities: Be careful where the currents are strong.

SARDINE RUN SOUTH AFRICA

Climate: Warm temperate. Stormy with rapid drops from 30–10°C (86–50°F) in winter; strong winds and high surf can prevent you going to sea for days.

Best time to go and how to get there:
June, though local operators suggest May–July. International links to Durban in the north and feeder airlines to East London in the south.

Vehicle-hire at both airports. Roads are generally very good, except in the Wild Coast area. Operators generally arrange either ground transportation or charter flights into the area of operation. Hiring a vehicle and driving is an option. In the Wild Coast area, mobile phone, good spare tyre and tools are a must for driving this route.

Note: Never drive after dark in the Wild Coast area.

Water temperature: 15–25°C (59–77°F); sardines generally not seen until the water drops below 20°C (68°F).

Visibility: Highly variable, 2–20m (6–66ft).

Quality of corals and marine life: Generally abundant, but winter seas do not make for good opportunities for viewing anything other than large offshore pelagic animals.

Depth of dives: Generally 20m (66ft) or less.

Recompression (hyperbaric) chambers:
PORT ELIZABETH:
Contact Subtech Diving via their Durban Head Office on +27 31 2062073
and
EAST LONDON:
East London Private Hospital
32 Albany Street
Tel: +27 43 7223128
and
DURBAN:
St Augustine's Hospital
107 Chelmsford Road, Glenwood
Tel: +27 31 2685255.
Emergency medical response: +27 82 911 (Netcare 911) DAN members can contact DAN Hotline on +27 82 911.

Snorkelling: Occasional opportunities with dolphins, for example, but scuba often better for offshore dolphin encounters. Snorkelling is not recommended in bait balls as there is no way to escape if the sardines seek shelter around the diver (scuba divers can duck out the bottom of a bait ball). Snorkelling to a bait ball may also frighten off the diving birds, which help hold the ball in place.

Dive practicalities: Level of dive qualification required: you should be professional, or at least highly proficient.

SEA OF CORTEZ

Climate: 26–35°C (79–95°F), best June–October.

Best time to go and how to get there: March–October; air links to US, Mexico and UK. Dive resorts can arrange airport transfers.

Water temperature: 18–25°C (65–77°F), but a wet suit is needed for protection.

Visibility: 25–50m (80–165ft).

Quality of corals and marine life: Corals poor in the north, but very good deep-water gorgonian sea fans and golden cup corals in shaded areas. Marine life is excellent; wide variety of both Pacific and Caribbean species.

Depth of dives: 45m (150ft) on offshore seamounts; 18m–30m (60–99ft) on other dives.

Recompression (hyperbaric) chambers:
Diving Medicine of Mexico
24hr toll free +1 800 700 2666
and
LA PAZ:
Cabo San Lucas, B.C.S. Mexico
Tel: +52 612 123 36 66.

Snorkelling: Superb off Los Islotes and for open ocean encounters with passing dolphins.

Dive practicalities: Beginner–advanced. Full 3–5mm semi-dry wet suit or dry suit is required.

SEYCHELLES

Climate: 29°C (84°F), tropical, sporadic rain.

Best time to go and how to get there: For Whale Sharks, August to October. Air links to UK, Europe, SA, India and other destinations.

Water temperatures: 26–27°C (79–80°F).

Visibility: 10–20m (33–66ft) with some thermoclines that can be hazy.

Quality of corals and marine life: Good.

Depth of dives: 10–30m (33–100ft). Snorkel encounters are at less than 5m (16ft).

Recompression (hyperbaric) chamber:
MAHÉ:
Victoria Hospital, Mont Fleuri, Mahé
Tel: +248 388 000.

Snorkelling: Be comfortable in open water.

Dive practicalities: Sites where chance encounters occur often have strong currents and are for experienced divers only.

THAILAND

Climate: There are two main seasons:
Northeast monsoon: Best for beach resorts and islands off Thailand's western coastline. Wet and windy (some sunnier days) across the eastern coastline November–April when rough seas in the Gulf make many of the islands inaccessible. Some sites in the Gulf's easternmost regions bordering Cambodia, such as the Mu Koh Chang Marine National Park, are sheltered and have the same favourable season as those in the Andaman Sea.
Southwest monsoon: May–October. High winds, rain and big waves make most sites in the Andaman Sea inaccessible. Conditions can be harsh. Weather along the eastern coast is kinder and the Gulf's waters are calmer.

Best time to go and how to get there: All year, depending on region and seasonal monsoons. Thailand is well served by airlines.

Water temperatures: 27–31°C (80–88°F); some thermoclines much cooler.

Visibility: Andaman Sea, in the best season, 5–30m (16–100ft); Gulf, same during the best season but good visibility is less frequent.

Quality of corals and marine life: Good.

Recompression chambers:
PHUKET CITY:

Badalveda Diving Medicine Network
Bangkok Phuket Hospital
Tel: +66 01 9899482.
and
PATONG BEACH:
Hyperbaric Services of Thailand
Tel: +66 076342518/9; Fax: +66 076345051.
and
Gulf of Thailand (east coast): KOH TAO:
Badalveda Diving Medicine Centre
Tel: +66 077 456664.
and
KOH SAMUI:
Bangkok Samui Hospital
Located just outside Chaweng Beach
Tel: +66 077 429500; Fax: +66 077 429505.
and
BIG BUDDHA BEACH:
Hyperbaric Services of Thailand:
Tel: +66 077 427427; Fax: +66 077 427377.

Snorkelling: Good.

Dive practicalities: Generally suitable for all levels of divers. Hin Daeng and Mouang suited to advanced divers, or less skilled provided professionals lead the dive. A thin wet suit is usually adequate.

UNITED KINGDOM

Climate: Very changeable. Air temperatures are affected by the wind-chill factor. Summer is May–September and winter is October–April. Most divers use dry suits year round though some use thick semi-dry suits in summer.

Best time to go and getting there: year round if sheltered; summer only for offshore sites. High sun in summer gives greater light penetration into the water. A good system of airline links, road and rail systems and ferry services so all sites are easily reached.

Water temperature: Winter, 2–8°C (36–46°F); summer, depending on depth, 9–18°C (48–65°F). The west coast tends to be warmest; temperatures highest in late summer.

Visibility: Generally poor, from 2–20m

(6–65ft), depending on the site and weather.

Quality of marine life: Many sites are very good with a high density of bottom-dwelling species including anemones, crustaceans and nudibranchs (sea slugs). Small shoals of fish shelter from the current in the lee of the rocks, others occupy crevices.

Many species of pelagic fish, some exotic visitors in the Gulf Stream and some introduced, alien species from ship's ballast.

Depth of dives: From the surface to depths well beyond the accepted limits of sport or recreational technical diving. Diving too deep is a common problem so act sensibly.

Recompression (hyperbaric) chambers: There are many hyperbaric chambers in the UK, mostly in hospitals near to the coast but others are in inland cities because divers may develop problems associated with decompression after returning home. With most coastal chambers, the person in charge of the rescue or boat contacts the coastguard or police first.

Snorkelling: Not recommended in most places due to tidal currents and poor visibility, but it is done with Basking Sharks offshore (with boat cover).

Dive practicalities: Treat all diving with respect even on calm summer days. Tides can be vicious and the weather can change quickly. Most dives require slack water. Plan dives with knowledge of the local tides and weather forecasts or dive from a day-boat or live-aboard boat with a knowledgeable skipper.

Operators have most facilities and popular equipment, day and live-aboard boats carry all necessary safety equipment, but do not dive in a dry suit without the proper training.

WESTERN AUSTRALIA

Climate: South, 14–32°C (57–90°F), north 30–34°C (86–92°F). There are two distinct seasonal variations – a southern hot summer, autumn, wet winter, spring; and a northern humid, wet and dry season. There are occa-

sional tropical cyclones in the wet season in north-western Australia.

Best time to go and how to get there: Peak season for Whale Sharks at Ningaloo Reef is April–June; limited, specialist live-aboard charters to the Rowley Shoals in October. Air links between Perth and other centres, or by road on the outback coastal highway.

Water temperatures: 19–26°C (66–80°F), with the warmest areas to the north.

Visibility: Sometimes poor, but up to 30m (100ft). Often if poor at one site it's better at a more protected site nearby. Exceptional at Rowley Shoals, reliably 40m (130ft).

Quality of corals and marine life: Corals and marine life are abundant in the central and northern areas. Pelagics include Whale Sharks, Manta Rays, and other sharks, tuna and trevallies. Big pelagics are guaranteed on wall dives at the Rowley Shoals.

Depth of dives: 18–30m (55–100ft)

Recompression (hyperbaric) chamber: FREEMANTLE:
Fremantle Hospital
Alma Street
Tel: +08 9431 3333
Note: A diver suffering decompression illness in the north of the State will be flown to Perth by the Royal Flying Doctor Service.

Snorkelling: Only snorkelling skills are required on Ningaloo Reef Whale Shark and manta tours. Operators teach the basic skills where necessary.

Dive practicalities: Only snorkelling and fin-kick skills are required on Ningaloo Reef Whale Shark and manta tours. Scuba certification to at least 18m (60ft) is required for the reef dives off the coast and islands. The more advanced 30m (100ft) certification is suggested for the Rowley Shoals, with Nitrox refills available for those with the correct qualification.

SPECIES: COMMON AND SCIENTIFIC NAMES

African (previously Jackass) Penguin
 (*Spheniscus demersus*)

Amberjack family (*Carangidae*)

Angelfish (*Pomocanthus imperator*)

Anthias (*Anthias* spp.)

Atlantic Bottlenose Dolphin (*Tursiops truncatus*)

Atlantic Spotted Dolphin (*Stenella frontalis*)

Atlantic White-sided Dolphin (*Lagenorhynchus acutus*)

Australian Sea Lion (*Neophoca cinerea*)

Baird's Beaked Whale (*Beradius bairdii*)

Baleen whales (*Mysticeti* spp.)

Barracuda (*Sphyraenidae* spp.)

Basking Shark (*Cetorhinus maximus*)

Batfish (*Ogcocephalus cubifrons*)

Beluga Whale (*Delphinapterus leucas*)

Bigeye Thresher Shark (*Alopias superciliosus*)

Blacktip Reef Shark (*Carcharhinus melanopterus*)

Blacktip Shark (*Carcharhinus limbatus*)

Blainville's Beaked Whale (*Mesoplodon densirostris*)

Blue Marlin (*Makaira nigricans*)

Blue Shark (*Prionace glauca*)

Blue Whale (*Balaenoptera musculus*)

Blue-ringed Octopus (*Hapalochlaena lunulata*)

Bluntnose Six-gill Shark (*Hexanchus griseus*)

Bonito (*Sarda sarda*)

Bottlenose Dolphin (*Tursiops truncatus*)

Bryde's Whale (*Balaenoptera edeni*)

Bull (Zambezi) Shark (*Carcharhinus leucas*)

Bumphead Parrotfish (*Bolbometopon muricatum*)

Butterflyfish (*Chaetodon* spp.)

California Sea Lion (*Zalophus californianus*)

Cape Fur Seal or South African Fur Seal
 (*Arctocephalus pusillus*)

Caribbean Reef Shark (*Carcharhinus perezi*)

Cleaner Wrasse (*Labroides dimidiatus* and
 Labroides bicolor)

Clymene Dolphin (*Stenella clymene*)

Common Bottlenose Dolphin (*Tursiops truncatus*)

Common Dolphin (*Delphinus delphis*)

Common Thresher Shark (*Alopias vulpinus*)

Cookie-cutter Shark (*Isistius brasiliensis*)

Copper Shark (Bronze Whaler)
 (*Carcharhinus brachyurus*)

Crescent-tail Bigeyes (also known as Zaizer's Bigeyes)
 (*Priacanthus hamrur*)

Cubera Snapper (*Lutjanus cyanopterus*)

Cuttlefish (*Sepia* spp.)

Cuvier's Beaked Whale (*Ziphius cavirostris*)

Dense Beaked Whale (*Mesoplodon densirostris*)

Dogtooth tuna (*Gymnosarda unicolor*)

Dugong (*Dugong dugon*)

Dusky Shark (*Carcharhinus obscurus*)

Dwarf Minke Whale (*Balaenoptera acutorostrata*)

Dwarf Sperm Whale (*Kogia simus*)

Eagle Ray (*Aetobatus narinari*)

Elephant Seal (*Mirounga angustirostris*)

European Eel (*Anguilla anguilla*)

False Killer Whale (*Pseudorca crassidens*)

Fin Whale (*Balaenoptera physalus*)

Finless Porpoise (*Neophocaena phocaenoides*)

Flamboyant Cuttlefish (*Metasepia pfefferi*)

Flatback Turtle (*Natator depressus*)

Fraser's Dolphin (*Lagenodelphis hosei*)

Frigate bird (*Fregata minor*)

Frogfish (*Antennariidae* spp.)

Galápagos Shark (*Carcharhinus galapagensis*)

Gannet (*Sula bassanus*)

Garden Eel (*Gorgasia Sillneri*)

Gervais' Beaked Whale (*Mesoplodon europaeus*)

Giant Grouper (*Epinephelus lanceolatus*)

Giant Trevally (*Caranx ignobilis*)

Ginko-toothed Whale (*Mesoplodon ginkgodens*)

Golden Trevally (*Gnathanodon speciosus*)

Goliath Grouper (*Epinephelus itajara*)

Gorgonian Sea Fan (*Gorgonaceae*)

Great Barracuda (*Sphyraena barracuda*)

Great Hammerhead Shark (*Sphyrna mokarran*)

Great White Shark (*Carcharodon carcharias*)

Green Turtle (*Chelonia mydas*)

Greenland Shark (*Somniosus microcephalus*)

Grey Reef Shark (*Carcharhinidae amblyrhynchos*)

Grey Whale (*Eschrichtius robustus*)

Grouper (*Mycteroperca* spp.)

Guadalupe Fur Seal (*Arctocephalus townsendi*)

Harbour Porpoise (*Phocoena phocoena*)

Hawaiian Monk Seal (*Monachus schauinslandi*)

Hawksbill Turtle (*Eretmochelys imbricata*)

Horn Shark (*Heterodontus francisci*)

Horse-eye Jack (*Caranx latus*)

Humpback Whale (*Megaptera novaeangliae*)

Humphead (Napoleon) Wrasse (*Cheilinus undulatus*)

Indo-Pacific Humpbacked Dolphin

(*Sousa chinensis*)

Irrawaddy Dolphin (*Orcaella brevirostris*)

Kemp's Ridley Turtle (*Lepidochelys kempi*)

Killer Whale (*Orcinus orca*)

King Angelfish (*Holacanthus passer*)

Kingfish (*Seriola lalandi*)

Leatherback Turtle (*Dermochelys coriacea*)

Lemon Shark (*Negaprion brevirostris*)

Lionfish (*Pterois* spp.)

Loggerhead Turtle (*Caretta caretta*)

Longfin Bannerfish (*Heniochus acuminatus*)

Longfin Pilot Whale (*Globicephala melas*)

Longfin Tuna (Albacore) (*Thunnus alalunga*)

Longnose Hawkfish (*Oxycirrhites typus*)

Mackerel (*Orcynus thunnus*)

Mahi-Mahi (Dorado or Dolphinfish)
 (*Coryphaena hippurus*)

Mako Shark (*Isurus* spp.)

Manta Ray (*Manta birostris*)

Megamouth Shark (*Megachasma pelagios*)

Melon-headed Whale (*Peponocephala electra*)

Mimic Octopus (*Octopus* spp.)

Minke Whale (*Balaenoptera acutorostrata*)

Mobula Ray (*Mobula* spp.)

Moray Eel (*Muraenidae* spp.)

Northern Bottlenose Whale (*Hyperoodon ampullatus*)

Northern Elephant Seal (*Mirounga angustirostris*)

Northern Right Whale (*Eubalaena glacialis*)

Nudibranch (*Nudibranchia*)

Nurse Shark (*Ginglymostoma cirratum*)

Ocean Sunfish (*Mola mola*)

Oceanic Whitetip Shark (*Carcharhinus longimanus*)

Olive Ridley Turtle (*Lepidochelys olivacea*)

Orca (*Orcinus orca*)

Pacific Olive Ridley Turtle (*Lepidochelys olivacea*)

Pan-tropical Spotted Dolphin (*Stenella attenuata*)

Pan-tropical Spotted Spinner Dolphin
 (*Stenella longirostris*)

Pelagic Thresher Shark (*Alopias pelagicus*)

Pelican (*Elecanus erythrorhynchos*)

Pilot Fish (*Naucrates duclor*)

Pilot Whale (*Globicephala melaena*)

Porbeagle Shark (*Lamna nasus*)

Potato Grouper (also Potato Bass)
 (*Epinephelus tukula*)

Pufferfish (*Fugu rubripes*)

Pygmy Killer Whale (*Feresa attenuata*)

Pygmy Sea Horse (*Hippocampus bargibanti*)

Pygmy Sperm Whale (*Kogia breviceps*)

Pygmy Whale (*Caperea marginata*)

Rabbitfish (*Siganus virgatus*)

Raggedtooth Shark (Sand, Tiger or Grey Nurse
 Shark) (*Carcharias taurus*)

Rainbow Runner (*Elagatis bipinnulata*)

Red Snapper (*Lutjanus campechanus*)

Remora (*Remora remora*)

Right Whale (*Eubalaena* spp.)

Risso's Dolphin (*Grampus griseus*)

Rough-toothed Dolphin (*Steno bredanensis*)

Roundtailed Ocean Sunfish or Common Mola
 (*Mola mola*)

Sandbar Shark (*Carcharhinus plumbeus*)

Sargassumfish (*Histrio histrio*)

Scalloped Hammerhead Shark (*Sphyrna lewini*)

Sea Horse (*Hippocampus* spp.)

Sea Moth (Pegasidae)

Sei Whale (*Balaenoptera borealis*)

Sergeant Major (*Abudefduf saxatilis*)

Sharp-tailed Ocean Sunfish or *Mola-mola*
 (*Masturus lanceolatus*)

Sharptooth Lemon (also known as Sicklefin Lemon)
 Shark (*Negaprion acutidens*)

Shortfin Mako (*Isurus oxyrinchus*)

Shortfin Pilot Whale (*Globicephala macrorhynchus*)

Silky Shark (*Carcharhinus falciformis*)

Silvertip Shark (*Carcharhinus albimarginatus*)

Six-banded Angelfish (*Pomacanthus sexstriatus*)

Smooth Hammerhead Shark (*Sphyrna zygaena*)

Southern Stingray (*Dasyatis americana* or
 Amphotistius longus)

Sowerby's Beaked Whale (*Mesoplodon bidens*)

Spanish Dancers (*Hexabranchus sanguineus*)

Sperm Whale (*Physeter macrocephalus*)

Spinner Dolphin (*Stenella longirostris*)

Spinner Shark (*Carcharhinidae brevipinna*)

Spiny Lobster (*Panulirus interruptus*)

Spotted Raggedtooth (also Sand, Tiger and
 Grey Nurse) Shark (*Carcharias taurus*)

Starfish (Asteroidea)

Stingray (*Dasyatis americana*)

Stonefish (*Synanceia* spp.)

Striped Dolphin (*Stenella coeruleoalba*)

Surgeonfish (Acanthuridae)

Sweetlips (*Plectorhinchus albovittatus*)

Thresher Shark (*Alopias vulpinus*)

Tiger Shark (*Galeocerdo cuvier*)

Titan or Yellowmargin Triggerfish
 (*Pseudobalistes flavimarginatus*)

Trevally (*Caranx* spp.)

Triggerfish (*Abalistes stellaris*)

True's Beaked Whale (*Mesoplodon mirus*)

Tuna (also known as Yellowfin Tuna)
 (*Thunnus* spp.)

Wahoo (*Acanthocybium solanderi*)

Whale Shark (*Rhincodon typus*)

Whitebeak Dolphin (*Lagenorhynchus albirostris*)

Wobbegong Shark (*Orectolobus ornatus*)

Wrasse (*Cirrhilabrus* spp.)

Yellowtail Kingfish (*Seriola lalandi*)

FURTHER READING AND INFORMATION SOURCES

FURTHER READING:

Diving with Sharks by Jack Jackson, published by New Holland Publishers

Sardine Run Field Guide by Andrew Aitken, published by Natal Sharks Board, available from Ocean Planet, web site www.oceanplanet.co.za, e-mail drewaitken@oceanplanet.co.za

Drama on the High Seas by Doug Perrine, National Wildlife Magazine, Oct-Nov. 2004, vol. 42 no. 6 http://www.nwf.org/nationalwildlife/article.cfm? articleId=977=70 <http://www.nwf.org/national-alwildlife/article.cfm?articleId=977&issueId=70>

Diving Hawaii and Midway by Mike Severns and Pauline Fiene, © 2002 Periplus Editions
Sharks & Rays of Hawaii by Gerald L. Crow and Jennifer Crites, © 2002 Mutual Publishing

Fiji Korina Miller, R. Jones and Leonardo Pinheiro, © 2003 Lonely Planet Publications

Diving & Snorkeling Fiji by Casey Mahaney & Astrid Witte, Lonely Planet Publications © 2000.

Diving and Snorkeling Guide to Fiji by W Gregory Brown, © 1993 Pisces Books

VIDEOS:
The Greatest Shoal on Earth and *Feast of Predators* videos by Peter Lamberti, Aquavision TV Productions; can be purchased from library@aquavision.co.za or tel +27-11-807-4900

HYPERBARIC FACILITIES:
http://www.scuba-doc.com/listchmbr.htm

MEDICAL FACILITIES:
http://bupa.wordtravels.com/Travelguide/

DIVE WEBSITES:
http://www.diversalertnetwork.org
http://www.scubaduba.com/search/scuba-div

ing.php
http://asiadivesite.com
http://www.scuba-spot.com
http://www.topscubasites.com
http://www.scubatravel.co.uk

COUNTRY GUIDE TO WORLD'S DIPLOMATIC MISSIONS:
http://www.escapeartist.com/embassy1/embassy1.htm

THE WORLD'S AIRLINES:
http://jwa.janes.com
http://www.hotelstravel.com/airlines.html
http://www.123world.com/airlines

COUNTRY ACCOMMODATION GUIDE:
http://ase.net
http://www.hotel-base.com
http://www.worldhotelcentre.com
http://www.worldbackpackers.net/

INDEX

PHOTOGRAPHIC CREDITS

Copyright © in photographs rests with the following photographers and/or their agents as listed below. Key to Locations: t = top; tl = top left; tr = top right; b = bottom; bl = bottom left; l = left; r = right; c = centre.

Page	Loc	Credit
Cover		Bob Halstead
Front flap		Lawson Wood
Spine		Jeff Rotman Photography
Back cover	l	© Doug Perrine/SeaPics.com
Back cover	r	Lochman Transparencies (Geoff Taylor)
1		Lawson Wood
2		Photo Access
4-5		Jeff Rotman Photography
6-7		© C & M Fallows/SeaPics.com
8-9		© Masa Ushioda/SeaPics.com
10		Danja Köhler
11		© Mark Strickland/SeaPics.com
12		Geoff Spiby
13		Chris Fallows
15		Michael AW
16		© SeaPics.com
17		Geoff Spiby
18		Jack Jackson
19		Kevin Deacon
20-21		Lochman Transparences
22	l	© Doug Perrine/SeaPics.com
22	tr, br	Photo Access
23		© Doug Perrine/SeaPics.com
25		© Doug Perrine/SeaPics.com
26-27		Lawson Wood
28		© Amos Nachoum/SeaPics.com
29		© Doug Perrine/SeaPics.com
30		© James D. Watt/SeaPics.com
31	t	Lawson Wood;
31	b	Lochman Transparencies /Geoff Taylor
32		© Doug Perrine/SeaPics.com
33	l	© James D. Watt/SeaPics.com
33	r	Lawson Wood
34-35		Lawson Wood
36		Photo Access
37		© Doug Perrine/SeaPics.com
38-40	t	Lawson Wood
40	b	Photo Access
41		© David B. Fleetham/SeaPics.com
42		Stephen Wong & Takako Uno
43		© Ralf Kiefner/SeaPics.com
44		Stephen Wong & Takako Uno
45		© Doug Perrine/SeaPics.com
46		Photo Access
47-50		© Doug Perrine/SeaPics.com
48		© Andre Seale/SeaPics.com
49		© Roland Seitre/SeaPics.com
50		© Doug Perrine/SeaPics.com
51-53	t	Chris Fallows
53	b	Photo Access
54-55		Chris Fallows
56-57		Jeff Rotman Photography
58		Jack Jackson
59		© Doc White/SeaPics.com
60-61	t	Jeff Rotman Photography
61	b	Photo Access
62		Jeff Rotman Photography
63	l	Jack Jackson
63	r	© Doug Perrine/SeaPics.com
64-70		© Mark Strickland/SeaPics.com
65-66		© James D. Watt/SeaPics.com
67		© Ron & Valerie Taylor/SeaPics.com
68		© James D. Watt/SeaPics.com
69		© Masa Ushioda/SeaPics.com
70		© Paul Humann/SeaPics.com
71		Neil Hammerschlag - SHARK RESEARCHER, PEW INSTITUTE FOR OCEAN SCIENCE, UNIVERSITY OF MIAMI
72	t	Al Hornsby
72	b	Photo Access
73		Peter Pinnock
74	t	© Doug Perrine/SeaPics.com
75-77	t	© Doug Perrine/SeaPics.com
77	b	Photo Access
78		© Steve Drogin/SeaPics.com
79		© Masa Ushioda/SeaPics.com
80		© David B. Fleetham/SeaPics.com
81		Lawson Wood
82-84		Paul Lees
85		Michael AW
86-87		Peter & Margy Nicholas
88		© David B. Fleetham/SeaPics.com
89		Peter & Margy Nicholas
90		Neil Hammerschlag - SHARK RESEARCHER, PEW INSTITUTE FOR OCEAN SCIENCE, UNIVERSITY OF MIAMI
91		© Masa Ushioda/SeaPics.com
92-93		Photo Access
94		Jack Jackson
95		© Robert L. Pitman/SeaPics.com
96		Michael AW
97	t	© Ben Cropp/SeaPics.com
97	b	© Doug Perrine/SeaPics.com
98		© Peter Kragh/SeaPics.com
99		© Nigel Marsh/SeaPics.com
100		© Walt Stearns/SeaPics.com
101		Photo Access
102-105		Stephen Wong & Takako Uno
106		© Nigel Marsh/SeaPics.com
107		© Tim Calver/SeaPics.com
108-109		© Doug Perrine/SeaPics.com
110		Photo Access
111		© Mark Jones/SeaPics.com
112		© Doug Perrine/SeaPics.com
113-114	t	Neil Hammerschlag - SHARK RESEARCHER, PEW INSTITUTE FOR OCEAN SCIENCE, UNIVERSITY OF MIAMI
114	b	Photo Access
115		© Bruce Rasner/SeaPics.com
116		Jack Jackson
117		Photo Access
118-123		Bob Halstead
124		© Doug Perrine/SeaPics.com
125	t	Jack Jackson)
125	b	© Doug Perrine/SeaPics.com
126	t	© Doug Perrine/SeaPics.com
126	b	© Bob Cranston/SeaPics.com
127		Michael AW
128		© Masa Ushioda/SeaPics.com
129	t	© Joao Quaresma/SeaPics.com
129	b	Photo Access
130	t	Photo Access
130	b	© James D. Watt/SeaPics.com
131-132		Photo Access
133		© Avi Klapfer/SeaPics.com
134-136		Photo Access
137		© David B. Fleetham/SeaPics.com
138		© Bob Cranston/SeaPics.com
139		© Phillip Colla/SeaPics.com
140		Lawson Wood
141		© Kike Calvo/V&W/SeaPics.com
142		© Franco Banfi/SeaPics.com
143	t	Photo Access
143	b	© Phillip Colla/SeaPics.com
144		Chris Fallows
145		Jeff Rotman Photography